Henry M. (Henry Martyn) Storrs

Scripture Selections for Christmas, Easter and Times of Affliction

Henry M. (Henry Martyn) Storrs

Scripture Selections for Christmas, Easter and Times of Affliction

ISBN/EAN: 9783741178528

Manufactured in Europe, USA, Canada, Australia, Japa

Cover: Foto ©Thomas Meinert / pixelio.de

Manufactured and distributed by brebook publishing software
(www.brebook.com)

Henry M. (Henry Martyn) Storrs

Scripture Selections for Christmas, Easter and Times of Affliction

Scripture Selections

FOR

Christmas, Easter, and Times of Affliction.

Καὶ αὕτη ἐστὶν ἡ μαρτυρία, ὅτι ζωὴν αἰώνιον ἔδωκεν ἡμῖν ὁ θεός· καὶ αὕτη ἡ ζωὴ ἐν τῷ υἱῷ αὐτοῦ ἐστίν.

1 John 5 : 11.

American Tract Society,

No. 150 Nassau Street. New York.

IF any reader shall have faith strengthened, or comfort supplied, through the manifestation of the Son of God in these selections from his Holy Word, the Compiler will have a rich reward— over and above what has come to his own heart while making them for use in his pastoral work.

It may be well to add that, while the "natural order of Scripture" has been freely disregarded, and passages—even parts of sentences—have been brought together from remote places in the Bible, it is yet believed that "the mind of the Spirit" has been studiously regarded, and that an essential and vindicating unity will be recognized as running through them, fitly compacting what every joint supplieth toward a steadily progressive unfolding of the Great Theme.

H. M. S.

Orange, N. J., 1889.

SCRIPTURES FOR CHRISTMAS.

Comfort ye, comfort ye my people, saith your God. O Zion, that bringest good tidings, get thee up into the high mountain; O Jerusalem, that bringest good tidings, lift up thy voice with strength; lift it up, be not afraid; say unto the cities of Judah, Behold your God!

The voice of him that crieth in the wilderness, Prepare ye the way of the Lord, make straight in the desert a highway for our God. Behold, his reward is with him, and his work before him. Say ye to the daughter of Zion, Behold, thy salvation cometh; and the glory of the Lord shall be revealed, and all flesh shall see it together.

Let the heavens be glad, and let the earth rejoice: let the sea roar, and the fulness thereof: let the floods clap their hands: let the hills be joyful together: let the trees of the wood sing out at the presence of the Lord, because he cometh, he cometh to judge the earth: he shall judge the world with righteousness, and the people with his truth. He shall feed his flock like a shepherd; he shall gather the lambs with his arm, and carry them in his bosom, and shall gently lead those that are with young.

But thou, Bethlehem Ephratah, though thou be little among the thousands of Judah, yet out of thee shall he come forth whose goings have been from of old, from everlasting. And he shall stand and feed his flock in the strength of the Lord, in the majesty of the name of the Lord. He shall be called the Son of the Highest, and of his kingdom there shall be no end. Behold, a virgin shall be with child, and shall bring forth a son, and they shall call his name Emmanuel; which being interpreted, is, God with us.

O Lord our Lord, how excellent is thy name in all the earth! Out of the mouth of babes and sucklings hast thou ordained strength. My soul doth magnify the Lord, and my spirit hath rejoiced in God my Saviour. Through the tender mercy of our God the day-spring from on high hath visited us, to give light to them that sit in darkness and in the shadow of death; to guide our feet into the way of peace. Fear not: for behold, I bring you good tidings of great joy, which shall be to all people. For unto you is born this day, in the city of David, a Saviour, which is Christ the Lord.

Glory to God in the highest, and on earth peace, good will toward men. For his mercy is on them that fear him, from generation to generation. Praise ye the Lord.

INCARNATION.—ITS OBJECT.

God so loved the world that he gave his only begotten Son, that whosoever believeth in him should not perish, but have everlasting life. God was in Christ reconciling the world unto himself, sending his own Son in the likeness of sinful flesh and as an offering for sin. In this was manifested the love of God toward us, because that

3

God sent his only begotten Son into the world, that we might live through him. For God sent not his Son into the world to condemn the world, but that the world through him might be saved.

Herein is love, not that we loved God, but that he loved us, and sent his Son to be the propitiation for our sins. And we have known and believed the love that God hath to us. The record is that God hath given to us eternal life, and this life is in his Son. And we have seen and do testify that the Father sent the Son to be the Saviour of the world.

In the beginning was the Word, and the Word was with God, and the Word was God. And the Word was made flesh, and dwelt among us, full of grace and truth. No man hath seen God at any time; the only begotten Son, which is in the bosom of the Father, he hath declared him. For when the fulness of the time was come, God sent forth his Son, made of a woman, made under the law, to redeem them that were under the law, that we might receive the adoption of sons; being justified freely by his grace, through the redemption that is in Christ Jesus.

Behold what manner of love the Father hath bestowed upon us, that we should be called the sons of God: and because ye are sons, God hath sent forth the Spirit of his Son into your hearts, crying, Abba, Father! He that spared not his own Son, but delivered him up for us all, how shall he not with him also freely give us all things? For if children, then heirs; heirs of God, and joint-heirs with Christ; if so be that we suffer with him, that we may be also glorified together. Wherefore thou art no more a servant, but a son; and if a son, then an heir of God.

That which was from the beginning, which we have heard, which we have seen with our eyes, which we have looked upon, and our hands have handled, of the Word of life which was with the Father, and was manifested unto us, declare we unto you, that ye may have fellowship with the Father, and with his Son Jesus Christ.

RECORD OF THE BIRTH.

Now the birth of Jesus Christ was on this wise: The angel Gabriel was sent from God unto a virgin espoused to a man, whose name was Joseph, of the house of David; and the virgin's name was Mary. And the angel said unto her, Hail, highly favored, the Lord is with thee: blessed art thou among women. Fear not, Mary, for thou hast found favor with God. And behold, thou shalt conceive and bring forth a son, and shalt call his name Jesus. Then said Mary unto the angel, How shall this be, seeing I know not a man? And the angel answered and said unto her, The Holy Ghost shall come upon thee, and the power of the Highest shall overshadow thee: therefore also that holy thing which shall be born of thee shall be called the Son of God.

And it came to pass, when Mary was espoused to Joseph, before they came together, she was found with child of the Holy Ghost. Then Joseph her husband, being a just man, and not willing to make her a public example, was minded to put her away privily. But while he thought on these things, behold, the angel of the Lord appeared unto him in a dream, saying, Joseph, thou son of David, fear not to take unto thee Mary thy wife: for that which is conceived in her is of the Holy Ghost. And she shall bring forth a son, and thou shalt call his name Jesus: for he shall save his people from their sins. Then Joseph, being raised from sleep, did as the angel of the Lord had bidden him, and took unto him his wife, and knew her not till she had brought forth her first-born son.

And it came to pass in those days, that there went out a decree from Cesar Augustus, that all the world should be taxed. And all went to be taxed, every one into his own city. And Joseph also went up from Galilee, out of the city of Nazareth, into Judea, unto the city of David, which is called Bethlehem, to be taxed with Mary his espoused wife, being great with child. And so it was, that while they were there, the days were accomplished, and she brought forth her first-born son, and wrapped him in swaddling-clothes, and laid him in a manger, because there was no room for them in the inn.

ATTESTING WITNESSES.
I. Angels and Shepherds.

And there were in the same country shepherds abiding in the field, keeping watch over their flock by night. And lo, the angel of the Lord came upon them, and the glory of the Lord shone round about them; and they were sore afraid. And the angel said unto them, Fear not: for, behold, I bring you good tidings of great joy, which shall be to all people. For unto you is born this day in the city of David, a Saviour, which is Christ, the Lord. And this shall be a sign unto you: ye shall find the babe wrapped in swaddling-clothes, lying in a manger. And suddenly there was with the angel a multitude of the heavenly host, praising God, and saying,

GLORY TO GOD IN THE HIGHEST, AND ON EARTH PEACE, GOOD WILL TOWARD MEN.

And it came to pass, as the angels were gone away from them into heaven, the shepherds said one to another, Let us now go even unto Bethlehem, and see this thing which is come to pass, which the Lord hath made known unto us. And they came with haste, and found Mary and Joseph, and the babe lying in a manger. And when they had seen it, they made known abroad the saying which was told them concerning this child. And the shepherds returned, glorifying and praising God for all the things that they had heard and seen, as it was told unto them. And all they that heard wondered at those things which were told them by the shepherds. But Mary kept all these things, and pondered them in her heart.

2. Waiting Temple-Saints.

And when eight days were accomplished for the circumcising of the child, his name was called Jesus, and they brought him to Jerusalem, to present him to the Lord; and, behold, there was a man in Jerusalem whose name was Simeon; and the same man was just and devout, waiting for the consolation of Israel: and the Holy Ghost was upon him. And it was revealed unto him by the Holy Ghost that he should not see death before he had seen the Lord's Christ. And he came by the Spirit into the temple: and when the parents brought in the child Jesus, to do for him after the custom of the law, then took he him up in his arms, and blessed God, and said:

Lord, now lettest thou thy servant depart in peace, according to thy word; for mine eyes have seen thy salvation, which thou hast prepared before the face of all people; a light to lighten the Gentiles, and the glory of thy people Israel.

And there was one Anna, a prophetess, of a great age, which departed not from the temple, but served with fastings and prayers night and day. And she coming in that instant, gave thanks likewise unto the Lord, and spake of him to all them that looked for redemption in Jerusalem.

3. Eastern Sages.

Now when Jesus was born in Bethlehem of Judea in the days of Herod the king, behold, there came wise men from the east, saying, Where is he that is born King of the Jews? for we have seen his star in the east, and are come to worship him.

When Herod the king had heard these things he was troubled, and all Jerusalem with him. And when he had gathered all the chief priests and scribes of the people together, he demanded of them where Christ should be born. And they said unto him, In Bethlehem of Judea; for thus it is written by the prophet: And thou Bethlehem, in the land of Juda, art not the least among the princes of Juda; for out of thee shall come a Governor, that shall rule my people Israel. Then Herod, when he had privily called the wise men, inquired of them diligently what time the star appeared. And he sent them to Bethlehem, and said, Go and search diligently for the young child; and when ye have found him, bring me word again, that I may come and worship him also. When they had heard the king, they departed; and, lo, the star, which they saw in the east, went before them, till it came and stood over where the young child was. When they saw the star, they rejoiced with exceeding great joy.

And when they were come into the house, they saw the young child with Mary his mother, and fell down, and worshipped him: and when they had opened their treasures, they presented unto him gifts: gold, and frankincense, and myrrh. And being warned of God that they should not return to Herod, they departed another way.

4. John, the Messenger.

There was a man sent from God, whose name was John. The same came for a witness, to bear witness of the Light. John bare witness of him, and cried, saying, This was he of whom I spake, He that cometh after me is preferred before me: for he was before me. And of his fulness have all we received, and grace for grace. No man hath seen God at any time; the only begotten Son, which is in the bosom of the Father, he hath declared him. And this is the record of John, when the Jews sent priests and Levites from Jerusalem to ask him, Who art thou?

I am the voice of one crying in the wilderness, Make straight the way of the Lord, as said the prophet Esaias. And I knew him not: but that he should be made manifest to Israel, therefore am I come baptizing with water. But he that cometh after me is mightier than I: he shall baptize you with the Holy Ghost, and with fire. I saw the Spirit descending from heaven like a dove, and it abode upon him. And I knew him not: but he that sent me to baptize with water, the same said unto me, Upon whom thou shalt see the Spirit descending, and remaining on him, the same is he which baptizeth with the Holy Ghost. And I saw and bare record that this is the Son of God.

5. The Father.

And it came to pass in those days, that Jesus came from Nazareth of Galilee, and was baptized of John in Jordan. And when he was baptized the heavens were opened unto him, and he saw the Spirit of God descending like a dove, and lighting upon him. And there came a voice from heaven, saying, Thou art my beloved Son, in whom I am well pleased.

And Jesus saith, Father, glorify thy name. Then came there a voice from heaven, saying, I have both glorified it, and will glorify it again. The people therefore that stood by and heard it said that it thundered: others said, An angel spake to him. Jesus answered and said, This voice came not because of me, but for your sakes. Ye sent unto John, and he bare witness unto the truth. But I have greater witness than that of John: the Father himself, which hath sent me, hath borne witness of me.

We have not followed cunningly-devised fables, when we made known unto you the power and coming of our Lord Jesus Christ, but were eyewitnesses of his majesty. For he received from God the Father honor and glory, when there came such a voice to him from the excellent glory, This is my beloved Son, in whom I am well pleased.

6. Christ Himself.

And the high priest arose, and said unto him, I adjure thee by the living God, that thou tell us whether thou be the Christ, the Son of God. Then said they all, Art thou then the Son of God? And he said unto them, Ye say that I am. And they said, What need we any further witness? for we ourselves have heard of his own mouth.

TRULY this was the Son of God.

BORN TO BE A PROPHET.

God, who at sundry times spake in time past unto the fathers by the prophets, hath in these last days spoken unto us by his Son Jesus Christ our Lord, which was made of the seed of

David according to the flesh; and declared to be the Son of God with power, according to the Spirit of holiness, by the resurrection from the dead: by whom we have received grace and apostleship, for obedience to the faith among all nations, for his name: a prophet mighty in deed and word before God and all the people. For Moses truly said unto the fathers, A prophet shall the Lord your God raise up unto you of your brethren; him shall ye hear in all things whatsoever he shall say unto you.

THEN spake Jesus, saying, I am the light of the world: he that followeth me shall not walk in darkness, but shall have the light of life, which lighteth every man that cometh into the world. I am come a light into the world, that whosoever believeth on me should not abide in darkness. Wherefore he saith, Awake, thou that sleepest, and arise from the dead, and Christ shall give thee light. To this end was I born, and for this cause came I into the world, that I should bear witness unto the truth. For he whom God hath sent speaketh the words of God. For the Father loveth the Son, and showeth him all things that himself doeth; and I speak to the world those things which I have heard of him: as my Father hath taught me, I speak these things. All things that I have heard of my Father I have made known unto you.

He that believeth on me, believeth not on me, but on him that sent me. I spake openly to the world, and in secret have I said nothing. I do nothing of myself; but as my Father hath taught me, I speak these things: for I proceeded forth and came from God; neither came I of myself, but he sent me. And this is the will of him that sent me, that every one which seeth the Son, and believeth on him, may have everlasting life. If a man keep my saying, he shall never see death. The words that I speak unto you, they are spirit, and they are life, and the word which ye hear is not mine, but the Father's which sent me. If ye had known me, ye should have known my Father also. I am the way, and the truth, and the life: no man cometh unto the Father, but by me. If ye continue in my word, ye shall know the truth, and the truth shall make you free. If the Son therefore shall make you free, ye shall be free indeed.

These things have I spoken unto you, being yet present with you. Nevertheless, I tell you the truth: It is expedient for you that I go away: for if I go not away, the Comforter will not come unto you; but if I depart, I will send him unto you. I have yet many things to say unto you, but ye cannot bear them now. But the Comforter, which is the Holy Ghost, whom the Father will send in my name, he shall teach you all things, and bring all things to your remembrance, whatsoever I have said unto you. When he, the Spirit of truth, is come, he will guide you into all truth.

O RIGHTEOUS Father, the world hath not known thee: but I have manifested thy name unto the men which thou gavest me out of the world: for I have

given unto them the words which thou
gavest me; and they have received
them, and have known surely that I
came out from thee. And I have declared unto them thy name, and will
declare it: that the love wherewith
thou hast loved me may be in them,
and I in them.

LORD, to whom shall we go? Thou
hast the words of eternal life. And we
are sure that thou art that Christ, the
Son of the living God; and hast given
us an understanding, that we may
know him that is true.

And we are in him that is true, even
in his Son Jesus Christ. This is the
true God, and eternal life. Whosoever
abideth not in the teaching of Christ
hath not God.

IN the last day, that great day of the
feast, Jesus stood and cried, saying, If
any man thirst, let him come unto me
and drink. He that believeth on me,
as the scripture hath said, out of his
belly shall flow rivers of living water.

Many of the people therefore, when they heard this saying, said, Of a truth, this is the Prophet.

BORN TO BE A PRIEST.

This is a faithful saying, and worthy of all acceptation, that Christ Jesus came into the world to save sinners.

Wherefore, holy brethren, partakers of the heavenly calling, consider the Apostle and High Priest of our profession, Christ Jesus; who was faithful to him that appointed him. Though he were a Son, yet learned he obedience by the things which he suffered; and being made perfect, he became the author of eternal salvation unto all them that obey him.

No man taketh this honor unto himself, but he that is called of God. So also Christ glorified not himself to be made a high priest; but he that said unto him, Thou art my Son, to-day have I begotten thee, saith also in another place, The Lord sware, and will not repent, Thou art a priest for

ever; called of God, this word of the
oath made the Son a high priest, con-
secrated forevermore, not after the law
of a carnal commandment, but after
the power of an endless life. And because he continueth ever, he hath an
unchangeable priesthood. Wherefore
he is able also to save them to the
uttermost that come unto God by him,
seeing he ever liveth to make intercession for them.

And if any man sin, we have an
advocate with the Father, Jesus Christ
the righteous. For Christ is entered
into heaven itself, now to appear in
the presence of God for us. Neither
by the blood of goats and calves, but
by his own blood, he entered in once
into the holy place, having obtained
eternal redemption.

But every high priest is ordained
to offer gifts and sacrifices: wherefore
it is of necessity that this man have
somewhat also to offer. Wherefore
when he cometh into the world, he
saith, Sacrifice and offering thou
wouldest not, but a body hast thou .
prepared me. Lo, I come to do thy

21

will, O God. By the which will we are sanctified through the offering of the body of Jesus Christ, who his own self bare our sins in his own body on the tree.

And he is the propitiation for our sins: and not for ours only, but also for the sins of the whole world. For ye know that ye were not redeemed with corruptible things, as silver and gold, but with the precious blood of Christ, as of a lamb without blemish and without spot: the Lamb of God, which taketh away the sin of the world: wounded for our transgressions, bruised for our iniquities, and he bare the sin of many, and made intercession for the transgressors.

But we see Jesus, who thought it not robbery to be equal with God, made lower than the angels, for the suffering of death, that he by the grace of God should taste death for every man. Forasmuch then as the children are partakers of flesh and blood, he also himself likewise took part of the same; in all things made like unto his brethren, that he might be a merciful and faithful high priest, to make reconciliation for the sins of the people.

Seeing then that we have a great high priest, that is passed into the heavens, Jesus the Son of God, let us hold fast our profession. For we have not a high priest which cannot be touched with the feeling of our infirmities; but was in all points tempted like as we are, yet without sin. Let us therefore come boldly unto the throne of grace, that we may obtain mercy and find grace to help in time of need.

For such an high priest became us, who is holy, harmless, undefiled, separate from sinners, and made higher than the heavens: who needeth not daily to offer up sacrifice, for by one offering he hath perfected for ever them that are sanctified. And after he had offered one sacrifice for sins, he for ever sat down on the right hand of God; from henceforth expecting till his enemies be made his footstool.

Worthy is the Lamb that was slain to receive power, and riches, and wisdom, and strength, and honor, and glory, and blessing; for thou wast slain, and hast redeemed us to God by thy blood, out of every kindred, and tongue, and people, and nation; and hast made us unto our God kings and priests: and we shall reign on the earth.

BORN TO BE A KING.

We have such an high priest, who is set on the right hand of the throne of the Majesty in the heavens. For God hath appointed his Son heir of all things, by whom also he made the worlds; who being the brightness of his glory, and the express image of his person, and upholding all things by the word of his power, when he had by himself purged our sins, sat down on the right hand of the Majesty on high. For when he bringeth the First-begotten into the world he saith: Thy kingdom is an everlasting kingdom, and thy dominion endureth throughout all generations. I will be to him a Father, and he shall be to me a Son: let all the angels of God worship him. I will make him my first-born, higher than the kings of the earth, King of kings, and Lord of lords. Thy throne, O God, is for ever and ever; the sceptre of thy kingdom is a right sceptre. Thou hast loved righteousness, and hated iniquity, therefore God, thy God, hath anointed thee with the oil of gladness above thy fellows. Thou, Lord, in the beginning hast laid the foundation of the earth, and the heavens are the works of thine hands. They shall perish, but thou remainest; and they all shall wax old as doth a garment, and as a vesture shalt thou fold them up, and they shall be changed; but thou art the same, and thy years shall not fail. Sit on my right hand, until I make thine enemies thy footstool.

Being in the form of God, he was made in the likeness of men: and being found in fashion as a man, he humbled himself, and became obedient unto death, even the death of the cross. Wherefore God also hath highly exalted him, and given him a name which is above every name: that at the name of Jesus every knee should bow, of things in heaven, and in earth, and under the earth; and that every tongue should confess that Jesus Christ is Lord, to the glory of God the Father.

MY HEART is inditing a good matter: I speak of the things which I have made touching the King; my tongue is the pen of a ready writer. Thou art fairer than the children of men; grace is poured into thy lips: therefore God hath blessed thee for ever. Gird thy sword upon thy thigh, O most mighty, with thy glory and thy majesty. And in thy majesty ride prosperously because of truth and meekness and righteousness.

Behold a King shall reign in righteousness, and a Man shall be as a hiding-place from the wind, and a covert from the tempest; as rivers of water in a dry place; as the shadow of a great rock in a weary land. The work of righteousness shall be peace; and the effect of righteousness, quietness and assurance for ever. Blessed be the King that cometh in the name of the Lord; peace in heaven, and glory in the highest.

Behold, the days come, saith the Lord, that I will perform that good thing which I have promised. I will raise unto David a righteous Branch, and a King shall reign and prosper, and shall execute judgment and justice in the earth. Thine eyes shall see the King in his beauty: and this is his name whereby he shall be called, the Lord our righteousness.

Behold the man, whose name is the Branch: he shall bear the glory, and shall sit and rule upon his throne; and he shall be a priest upon his throne. He shall be called the Son of the Highest; and of his kingdom there shall be no end.

And Jesus said, What think ye of Christ? Whose son is he? How doth David by the Holy Ghost call him Lord, saying, The Lord said unto my Lord, Sit thou on my right hand, till I make thine enemies thy footstool? If David then call him Lord, how is he his son?

THEN all the chief priests and elders of the people took counsel against Jesus to put him to death. And when they had bound him, they led him away, and delivered him to Pontius Pilate the governor. And they began to accuse him, saying, We found this fellow perverting the nation, and forbidding to give tribute to Cæsar, saying that he himself is Christ a King. Pilate therefore said unto him, Art thou a King then? Jesus answered, I am a King. My kingdom is not of this world: if my kingdom were of this world, then would my servants fight, that I should not be delivered to the Jews: but now is my kingdom not from hence. To this end was I born, and for this cause came I into the world, that I should bear witness unto the truth. Every one that is of the truth heareth my voice.

When Pilate knew that he belonged unto Herod's jurisdiction, he sent him to Herod. And Herod with his men of war set him at nought, and mocked him, and arrayed him in a gorgeous robe, and sent him again to Pilate.

Then said Pilate to the chief priests, and to the people, I have found no cause of death in him; no, nor yet Herod; I will therefore chastise him, and let him go. And they were instant with loud voices, requiring that he might be crucified: and the voices of them and of the chief priests prevailed. And Pilate gave sentence that it should be as they required.

Why did the heathen rage, and the people imagine vain things? The kings of the earth stood up, and the rulers were gathered together against the Lord, and against his Christ. For of a truth against thy holy child Jesus, whom thou hast anointed, both Herod and Pontius Pilate, with the Gentiles, and the people of Israel were gathered together, saying, Let us break their bands asunder, and cast away their cords from us.

He that sitteth in the heavens shall laugh: the Lord shall have them in derision. Then shall he speak unto them in his wrath, and vex them in his sore displeasure. Yet have I set my King upon my holy hill of Zion. I will de-

clare the decree: the Lord hath said
unto me, Thou art my Son; this day
have I begotten thee. Ask of me, and
I shall give thee the heathen for thine
inheritance, and the uttermost parts of
the earth for thy possession. Be wise
now, therefore, O ye kings; be in-
structed, ye judges of the earth. Serve
the Lord with fear, and rejoice with
trembling. Kiss the Son, lest he be
angry, and ye perish from the way,
when his wrath is kindled but a little.
Blessed are all they that put their trust
in him.

How beautiful upon the mountains
are the feet of him that bringeth good
tidings, that publisheth peace; that
bringeth good tidings of good, that
publisheth salvation; that saith unto
Zion, Thy God reigneth! Behold, thy
King cometh unto thee: he is just, and
having salvation; lowly, and riding
upon an ass, and upon a colt the foal
of an ass. Hosanna; blessed is the
King that cometh in the name of the
Lord!

And Jesus, when he had found a
young ass, sat thereon; as it is written,

Fear not, daughter of Zion: behold, thy King cometh, sitting on an ass's colt. Sing, O daughter of Zion; the King of Israel, even the Lord, is in the midst of thee. Fear thou not, the Lord thy God in the midst of thee is mighty; he will save, he will rejoice over thee with joy; he will rest in his love, he will joy over thee with singing. Behold, the Lord God will come with strong hand, and his arm shall rule for him: behold, his reward is with him, and his work before him. And his feet shall stand in that day upon the Mount of Olives, which is before Jerusalem on the east, and it shall be in that day that living waters shall go out from Jerusalem. And the Lord shall be King over all the earth: in that day shall there be one Lord, and his name one. He shall have dominion from sea to sea, and from the river unto the ends of the earth.

In his days shall the righteous flourish, and abundance of peace so long as the moon endureth. The kings of Tarshish and of the isles shall bring presents, the kings of Sheba and Seba shall offer gifts. Yea, all kings shall fall down before him, all nations shall serve him. For he shall deliver the needy when he crieth; the poor also, and him that hath no helper. He shall not cry, nor lift up, nor cause his voice to be heard in the street. A bruised reed shall he not break. He shall not fail nor be discouraged, till he have set judgment in the earth. The isles shall wait for his law. The mountains shall bring peace to the people. He shall spare the poor and needy, and shall save the souls of the needy. He shall redeem their soul from deceit and violence, and precious shall their blood be in his sight. He shall judge the poor of the people, and shall break in pieces the oppressor; prayer also shall be made for him continually, and daily shall he be praised. His name shall endure for ever: his name shall be continued as long as the sun, and men shall be blessed in him: all nations shall call him blessed.

Sing and rejoice, O daughter of Zion: for, lo, I come, and I will dwell

in the midst of thee, saith the Lord.
Sing, O heavens; and be joyful, O
earth; and break forth into singing,
O mountains, for the Lord hath comforted his people; and the Redeemer
shall come to Zion, and thou shalt
know that I the Lord am thy Saviour
and thy Redeemer. Therefore the
redeemed of the Lord shall return, and
come with singing unto Zion; and
everlasting joy shall be upon their
head: they shall obtain gladness and
joy; and sorrow and mourning shall
flee away.

ARISE, shine; for thy light is come,
and the glory of the Lord is risen upon
thee. For behold, the darkness shall
cover the earth, and gross darkness
the people: but the Lord shall arise
upon thee, and his glory shall be seen
upon thee. The people that walked in
darkness have seen a great light: they
that dwell in the land of the shadow
of death, upon them hath the light
shined. For unto us a Child is born,
unto us a Son is given: and the government shall be upon his shoulder:

33

and his name shall be called Wonderful, Counsellor, the mighty God, the everlasting Father, the Prince of Peace. Of the increase of his government and peace there shall be no end.

Say to them that are of a fearful heart, Be strong, fear not; behold, your God will come and save you. Then the eyes of the blind shall be opened, and the ears of the deaf shall be unstopped; then shall the lame man leap as a hart, and the tongue of the dumb sing: for in the wilderness shall waters break out, and streams in the desert.

JOHN sent unto Jesus, saying, Art thou he that should come?

And in that same hour he cured many of their infirmities and plagues, and of evil spirits; and unto many that were blind he gave sight. Then Jesus answering, said, Go your way, and tell John what things ye have seen and heard: how that the blind see, the lame walk, the lepers are cleansed, the deaf hear, the dead are raised, to the poor the gospel is preached.

And they brought young children to him, that he should touch them: and he took them up in his arms, put his hands upon them, and blessed them, and said, Suffer the little children to come unto me, and forbid them not: for of such is the kingdom of God. Whosoever shall not receive the kingdom of God as a little child, he shall not enter therein. I am among you as he that serveth. And I appoint unto you a kingdom, as my Father hath appointed unto me. It is a faithful saying: If we suffer, we shall also reign with him. For the Son of man is come to seek and to save that which was lost.

And Jesus returned in the power of the Spirit into Galilee, and went into the synagogue on the sabbath-day, and stood up for to read. And when he had opened the book, he found the place where it was written, The Spirit of the Lord is upon me, because he hath anointed me to preach the gospel to the poor; he hath sent me to heal the broken-hearted, to preach deliverance to the captives, and recovering of sight to the blind, to set at liberty them that are bruised; to preach the acceptable year of the Lord. And the eyes of all them that were in the synagogue were fastened on him. And he began to say unto them, This day is this scripture fulfilled in your ears.

I WILL extol thee, my God, O King; and I will bless thy name for ever and ever. And thy saints shall bless thee. They shall speak of the glory of thy kingdom, and talk of thy power. The kingdoms of this world are become the kingdoms of our Lord, and of his Christ: and he shall reign for ever and ever. For thou hast been a strength to the poor, a strength to the needy in his distress, a refuge from the storm, a shadow from the heat, when the blast of the terrible ones is as a storm against the wall. And it shall be said in that day, Lo, this is our God: we have waited for him, and he will save us: this is the Lord: we have waited for him, we will be glad and rejoice in his salvation. For the Lord is our Judge, the Lord is our Lawgiver, the Lord is our King; he will save us.

AND I heard a great voice out of heaven saying, Behold, the tabernacle of God is with men, and he will dwell with them, and they shall be his people, and God himself shall be with them, Immanuel, and be their God. And God shall wipe away all tears from their eyes; and there shall be no more death, neither sorrow, nor crying, neither shall there be any more pain: for the former things are passed away. And he that sat upon the throne said, Behold, I make all things new. To him that overcometh will I grant to sit with me in my throne, even as I also overcame, and am set down with my Father in his throne. I am Alpha and Omega, the beginning and the ending, saith the Lord, which is, and which was, and which is to come, the Almighty. He that overcometh shall inherit all things; and I will be his God, and he shall be my son. Lord, now lettest thou thy servant depart in peace, according to thy word: for mine eyes have seen thy salvation, which thou hast prepared before the face of all people; a light to lighten the

Gentiles, and the glory of thy people Israel.

WHEN the Son of man shall come in his glory, and all the holy angels with him, then shall he sit upon the throne of his glory: and before him shall be gathered all nations: and he shall separate them one from another, as a shepherd divideth his sheep from the goats: and he shall set the sheep on his right hand, but the goats on the left. For the Father judgeth no man, but hath committed all judgment unto the Son: that all men should honor the Son, even as they honor the Father. Then shall the King say unto them on his right hand, Come, ye blessed of my Father, inherit the kingdom prepared for you from the foundation of the world: for I was an hungered, and ye gave me meat; I was thirsty, and ye gave me drink; I was a stranger, and ye took me in; naked, and ye clothed me; I was sick, and ye visited me; I was in prison, and ye came unto me. Then shall the righteous answer him, saying, Lord, when saw we thee an hungered, and fed thee? or thirsty, and gave thee drink? When saw we thee a stranger, and took thee in? or naked, and clothed thee? Or when saw we thee sick, or in prison, and came unto thee? And the King shall answer and say unto them, Verily I say unto you, inasmuch as ye have done it unto one of the least of these my brethren, ye have done it unto me.

THEN cometh the end, when he shall have delivered up the kingdom to God, even the Father; when he shall have put down all rule, and all authority and power. And when all things shall be subdued unto him, then shall the Son also himself be subject unto him that put all things under him, that God may be all in all.

UNTO him that loved us, and washed us from our sins in his own blood, and hath made us kings and priests unto God and his Father, to him be glory and dominion for ever and ever. Amen.

NOW unto the King eternal, immortal, invisible, the only wise God, who hath delivered us from the power of darkness, and hath translated us into the kingdom of his dear Son, be honor and glory for ever and ever. Amen.

SCRIPTURES FOR EASTER.

PRELUDE.

THE LORD IS RISEN!

Grace be to you, and peace, from God our Father, and from the Lord Jesus Christ, who is the first begotten of the dead, and the ruler of the kings of the earth. Unto him that loved us, and washed us from our sins in his own blood, and hath made us kings and priests unto God and his Father: to him be glory and dominion for ever and ever. Amen.

Fear not ye: for I know that ye seek Jesus, which was crucified; he is risen; he is not here. Why seek ye the living among the dead? For Christ, being raised from the dead, dieth no more; death hath no more dominion over him. Fear not, he said, I am the first and the last: I am he that liveth, and was dead; and, behold, I am alive for evermore. Amen.

Thus it behoved Christ to suffer, and to rise from the dead the third day: whom God hath raised up, having loosed the pains of death; because it was not possible that he should be holden of it.

The prophets and Moses did say that Christ should suffer, and that he should be the first that should rise from the dead, and should show light unto the people, and to the Gentiles. And we declare unto you glad tidings, how that the promise which was made unto the fathers, God hath fulfilled unto us their children, in that he hath raised up Jesus. Him hath God exalted with his right hand to be a Prince and a Saviour, to give repentance to Israel, and forgiveness of sins. Unto you God, having raised up his Son Jesus, sent him to bless you, in turning away every one of you from his iniquities. Be it known unto you therefore, men and brethren, that through this man is preached unto you the forgiveness of sins; and whosoever among you feareth God, to you is the word of this salvation sent.

O my God, how great is thy goodness, which thou hast laid up for them

2

that fear thee. O Lord, thou hast brought up my soul from the grave; thou wilt show me the path of life. The sorrows of death compassed me, and the pains of hell gat hold upon me: but thou hast delivered my soul from death. The Lord was my stay; he delivered me, because he delighted in me. In thee, O Lord, do I put my trust; for with thee is the fountain of life; I shall be satisfied, when I awake, with thy likeness. Therefore my heart is glad, and my flesh also shall rest in hope. For if we believe that Jesus died and rose again, even so them also which sleep in Jesus will God bring with him. But every man in his own order: Christ the first-fruits; afterward they that are Christ's, when he shall come to be glorified in his saints.

Jesus lifted up his eyes to heaven, and said, Father, the hour is come; glorify thou me with thine own self, with the glory which I had with thee before the world was. I will that they also whom thou hast given me be with me where I am, that they may behold my glory.

3

Ought not Christ to have suffered these things, and to enter into his glory? But if we be dead with Christ, we believe that we shall also live with him.

Blessed be the God and Father of our Lord Jesus Christ, the Father of glory, who hath raised him from the dead, and set him at his own right hand in the heavenly places, far above all principality, and power, and might, and dominion, and every name that is named, not only in this world, but also in that which is to come: and hath put all things under his feet. Wherefore he saith, Thou hast ascended on high, thou hast led captivity captive: thou hast received gifts for men; yea, for the rebellious also, that the Lord God might dwell among them. Lift up your heads, O ye gates; and be ye lift up, ye everlasting doors; and the King of glory shall come in. Who is this King of glory? The Lord, strong and mighty. Lift up your heads, O ye gates; even lift them up, ye everlasting doors; and the King of glory shall come in.

Blessed be the God and Father of our Lord Jesus Christ, which according to his abundant mercy hath begotten us again unto a lively hope by the resurrection of Jesus Christ from the dead, who is gone into heaven, and is set down at the right hand of the throne of God: angels, and authorities, and powers being made subject unto him.

Now the God of peace, that brought again from the dead our Lord Jesus, that great Shepherd of the sheep, through the blood of the everlasting covenant, make you perfect in every good work to do his will, working in you that which is wellpleasing in his sight, through Jesus Christ; to whom be glory for ever and ever. Amen. Grace be with you all. Praise ye the Lord.

FORESHADOWINGS.

O God, be not far from me: O my God, make haste for my help.

The assembly of the wicked have enclosed me: they pierced my hands and my feet. They gave me also gall for my meat; and in my thirst they gave me vinegar to drink. They part my garments among them, and cast lots upon my vesture. All they that see me laugh me to scorn: they shoot out the lip, they shake the head, saying, He trusted on the Lord that he would deliver him: let him deliver him, seeiug he delighted in him. I trusted in thee, O Lord. I said, Thou art my God, into thy hand I commit my spirit.

My God, my God, why hast thou forsaken me? But be not thou far from me, O Lord; O my strength, haste thee to help me. I am counted with them that go down into the pit: cast off among the dead, like the slain that lie in the grave, whom thou rememberest no more. Wilt thou show wonders to the dead? Shall the dead arise and praise thee?

AWAKE, O sword, against my Shepherd, and against the man that is my fellow, saith the Lord of Hosts: smite the Shepherd, and the sheep shall be scattered.

O, my Father, if it be possible, let this cup pass from me: nevertheless, not as I will, but as thou wilt. ˙ The cup which my Father hath given me, shall I not drink it?

All we, like sheep, have gone astray; and the Lord hath laid on him the iniquity of us all, yet he opened not his mouth: he is brought as a lamb to the slaughter, and as a sheep before her shearers is dumb, so he openeth not his mouth. He is despised and rejected of men; a man of sorrows, and acquainted with grief. Surely he hath borne our griefs, and carried our sorrows: yet we did esteem him stricken, smitten of God, and afflicted.

And one shall say unto him, What are these wounds in thy hands? Then he shall answer, Those with which I was wounded in the house of my friends. But he was wounded for our transgressions, he was bruised for our iniquities, the chastisement of our peace was upon him, and with his stripes we are healed. He was numbered with the transgressors; and he bare the sin of many, and made intercession for the transgressors. He made his grave with the wicked, and with the rich in his death.

BUT God will redeem my soul from the power of the grave: yea, though I walk through the valley of the shadow of death, I will fear no evil: for thou art with me. Moreover also, my flesh shall rest in hope: because thou wilt not leave my soul in hell, neither wilt thou suffer thine Holy One to see corruption. Thy dead shall live: together with my dead body shall they arise. Awake and sing, ye that dwell in dust: for the earth shall cast out the dead, and many of them that sleep in the dust of the earth shall awake.

O Lord my God, I cried unto thee, and thou hast brought up my soul from the grave: thou hast delivered my soul from death. I will praise thee; for thou hast heard me, and art become my salvation. The stone which the builders refused is become the head of the corner. This is the Lord's doing; it is marvellous in our eyes. We will rejoice and be glad in it. Open to me the gates of righteousness: I will go into them, and I will praise the Lord. I shall not die, but live, and declare the works of the Lord. He restoreth my soul.

In that day shall this song be sung: Trust ye in the Lord for ever; for in the Lord Jehovah is everlasting strength. Praise ye the Lord.

FORESIGHT.

And it came to pass, when Jesus came into the coasts of Cesarea Philippi, as he was alone praying, he asked his disciples, saying, Whom say ye that I am? And Simon Peter answered and said, Thou art the Christ, the Son of the living God. And he straitly charged them, and commanded them to tell no man that thing, saying, The Son of man must suffer many things, and be rejected of the elders, and chief priests, and scribes, and be slain, and be raised the third day.

And after six days, Jesus taketh Peter, James, and John his brother, and bringeth them up into an high mountain apart, and was transfigured before them: and his face did shine as the sun, and his raiment was white as the light. And behold, there appeared unto them Moses and Elias in glory, and spake of his decease which he should accomplish at Jerusalem. And as they came down from the mountain, Jesus charged them, saying, Tell the vision to no man, until the Son of man be risen again from the dead.

From that time forth began Jesus to show unto his disciples, how that he must go unto Jerusalem, and suffer many things of the elders, and chief priests, and scribes, and be killed, and be raised again the third day. And while they abode in Galilee, Jesus said unto them, The Son of man shall be betrayed into the hands of men: and they shall kill him, and the third day he shall be raised again.

And Jesus going up to Jerusalem, took the twelve disciples apart in the way, and said unto them, Behold, we go up to Jerusalem; and the Son of man shall be betrayed unto the chief priests, and unto the scribes, and they shall condemn him to death, and shall deliver him to the Gentiles to mock, and to scourge, and to crucify him: and the third day he shall rise again. And I, if I be lifted up from the earth, will draw all men unto me. This he said, signifying what death he should die.

Then answered the Jews, and said unto him, What sign showest thou unto us, seeing that thou doest these things? Jesus answered and said unto them, Destroy this temple, and in three days I will raise it up. He spake of the temple of his body. When therefore he was risen from the dead, his disciples remembered that he had said this unto them.

THEN came the day of unleavened bread, when the passover must be killed. And when the hour was come, he sat down, and the twelve apostles with him. And he said unto them, With desire I have desired to eat this passover with you before I suffer. But behold, the hand of him that betrayeth me is with me on the table. All ye shall be offended because of me this night: for it is written, I will smite the Shepherd, and the sheep of the flock shall be scattered abroad. But after I am risen again, I will go before you into Galilee. And now I have told you before it come to pass, that, when it is come to pass, ye might believe.

And when they had sung an hymn, they went out into the mount of Olives, where was a garden, into the which he entered, and his disciples.

DEATH ACCOMPLISHED.

Judas then, having received a band of men and officers from the chief priests and Pharisees, cometh thither with lanterns, and torches, and weapons. Then all the disciples forsook him, and fled. Then the band, and the captain, and officers of the Jews took Jesus, and bound him, and led him away to the high priest.

When the morning was come, all the chief priests and elders of the people took counsel against Jesus to put him to death. And when they had bound him, they led him away, and delivered him to Pontius Pilate the governor. Then said Pilate unto them, Take ye him, and judge him according to your law. The Jews therefore said unto him, It is not lawful for us to put any man to death. Then said Pilate to the chief priests and to the people, I find no fault in this man. And the chief priests and scribes stood and vehemently accused him. And Pilate said, Behold, I, having examined him before you, have found no fault in this man, touching those things whereof ye accuse him. No, nor yet Herod: for I sent you to him; and, lo, nothing worthy of death is done unto him. I will therefore chastise him, and release him. But they cried, saying, Crucify, crucify him. And he said unto them the third time, Why, what evil hath he done? I have found no cause of death in him: I will therefore chastise him, and let him go. And they were instant with loud voices, requiring that he be crucified. And so Pilate, willing to content the people, delivered Jesus, when he had scourged him, to be crucified. And they took Jesus, and led him away. And he, bearing his cross, went forth into a place which is called Calvary, where they crucified him, and two others with him, on either side one, and Jesus in the midst.

Then said Jesus, Father, forgive them; for they know not what they do. And they parted his raiment, and cast lots. And it was about the sixth hour, and there was a darkness over all the earth until the ninth hour. And the sun was darkened, and the vail of the temple was rent in the midst. And at the ninth hour Jesus cried with a loud voice, saying, My God, my God, why hast thou forsaken me? After this, Jesus knowing that all things were now accomplished, that the scripture might be fulfilled, saith, I thirst: and they filled a sponge with vinegar, and put it to his mouth. When Jesus therefore had received the vinegar, he cried with a loud voice, It is finished: Father, into thy hands I commend my spirit; and having said thus, he bowed his head, and gave up the ghost.

14

AND when the even was come, Joseph of Arimathea, an honourable counsellor, which also waited for the kingdom of God, came, and went in boldly unto Pilate, and craved the body of Jesus. And Pilate marvelled if he. were already dead: and calling unto him the centurion, he asked him whether he had been any while dead. And when he knew it of the centurion, he gave the body to Joseph.

And there came also Nicodemus (which at the first came to Jesus by night) and brought a mixture of myrrh and aloes, about an hundred pound weight. Then took they the body of Jesus, and wound it in linen clothes with the spices, as the manner of the Jews is to bury. Now in the place where he was crucified there was a garden; and in the garden a new sepulchre, wherein was never man yet laid. There laid they Jesus therefore, and rolled a great stone to the door of the sepulchre, and departed. And the women also, which came with him from Galilee, followed after, and beheld the sepulchre, and how his body was laid.

And they returned, and prepared spices and ointments; and rested the sabbath-day, according to the commandment.

NOW the next day that followed the day of the preparation, the chief priests and Pharisees came together unto Pilate, saying, Sir, we remember that that deceiver said, while he was yet alive, After three days I will rise again. Command therefore that the sepulchre be made sure until the third day, lest his disciples come by night, and steal him away, and say unto the people, He is risen from the dead: so the last error shall be worse than the first. Pilate said unto them, Ye have a watch: go your way, make it as sure as ye can. So they went and made the sepulchre sure, sealing the stone, and setting a watch.

THE RESURRECTION.

In the end of the Sabbath, as it began to dawn toward the first of the week, behold, there was a great earthquake: for the angel of the Lord descended from heaven, and came and rolled back the stone from the door, and sat upon it. His countenance was like lightning, and his raiment white as snow. And for fear of him the keepers did shake, and became as dead men.

THE first of the week cometh Mary Magdalene early, when it was yet dark, unto the sepulchre, and seeth the stone taken away from the sepulchre. Then she runneth, and cometh to Simon Peter, and to the other disciple whom Jesus loved, and saith unto them, They have taken away the Lord out of the sepulchre, and we know not where they have laid him. Peter therefore went forth, and that other disciple, and came to the sepulchre. So they ran both together: and the other disciple did outrun Peter, and came first to the sepulchre. And he stooping down saw the linen clothes lying; yet went he not in. Then cometh Simon Peter following him, and went into the sepulchre, and seeth the linen clothes lie; and the napkin that was about his head, not lying with the linen clothes, but wrapped together in a place by itself. Then went in also that other disciple which came first to the sepulchre, and he saw, and believed. For as yet they knew not the scripture, that he must rise again from the dead. Then the disciples went away again unto their own home.

But Mary stood without at the sepulchre weeping: and as she wept she stooped down and looked into the sepulchre, and seeth two angels in white, sitting, the one at the head, and the other at the feet, where the body of Jesus had lain. And they say unto her, Woman, why weepest thou? She saith unto them, Because they have taken away my Lord, and I know not where they have laid him. And when she had thus said, she turned herself back, and saw Jesus standing, and knew not that it was Jesus. Jesus saith unto her, Woman, why weepest thou? whom seekest thou? She, supposing him to be the gardener, saith unto him, Sir, if thou have borne him hence, tell me where thou hast laid him, and I will take him away. Jesus saith unto her, Mary! She turned herself, and saith unto him, Rabboni, which is to say, Master. Jesus saith unto her, Touch me not: for I am not yet ascended to my Father: but go to my brethren, and say unto them, I ascend unto my Father and your Father, and to my God and your God.

Mary Magdalene came and told them that had been with him, as they mourned and wept, that she had seen the Lord, and that he had spoken these things unto her. And they, when they had heard that he was alive, and had been seen of her, believed not.

Now upon the first of the week, very early in the morning, the women also, which came with him from Galilee, came unto the sepulchre, bringing the spices which they had prepared, and certain others with them. And they found the stone rolled away from the sepulchre. And they entered in, and found not the body of the Lord Jesus. And it came to pass, as they were much perplexed thereabout, behold, two men stood by them in shining garments. And as they were afraid, and bowed down their faces to the earth, they said unto them, Why seek ye the living among the dead? Fear not ye: ye seek Jesus, which was crucified. He is not here: for he is risen, as he said. Come, see the place where the Lord lay. Remember how he spake unto you when he was yet in Galilee, saying, The Son of man must be delivered into the hands of sinful men, and be crucified, and the third day rise again. And go quickly, and tell his disciples that he is risen from the dead; and, behold, he goeth before you into Galilee; there shall ye see him: lo, I have told you.

And they remembered his words, and departed quickly from the sepulchre with fear and great joy, and did run to bring his disciples word. And as they went to tell his disciples, behold, Jesus met them, saying, All hail! And they came and held him by the feet, and worshipped him. Then said Jesus unto them, Be not afraid: go tell my brethren that they go into Galilee, and there shall they see me.

And they returned from the sepulchre, and told all these things unto the eleven, and to all the rest. It was Mary Magdalene, and Joanna, and Mary the mother of James, and other women that were with them, which told these things unto the apostles. And their words seemed to them as idle tales, and they believed them not.

Now when they were going, behold, some of the watch came into the city, and showed unto the chief priests all the things that were done. And when they were assembled with the elders, and had taken counsel, they gave large money unto the soldiers, saying, Say ye, his disciples came by night, and stole him while we slept. And if this come to the governor's ears, we will persuade him, and secure you. So they took the money, and did as they were taught; and this saying is commonly reported among the Jews until this day.

THE same day he appeared in another form unto two of them, as they walked, and went into the country. And it came to pass, as he sat at meat with them, he took bread, and blessed, and brake, and gave to them. And their eyes were opened, and they knew him; and he vanished out of their sight.

And they rose up the same hour, and returned to Jerusalem, and found the eleven gathered together, and them that were with them, saying, The Lord is risen indeed, and hath appeared to Simon; and they told what things were done in the way, and how he was known of them in breaking of bread; neither believed they them.

AND as they thus spake, Jesus himself stood in the midst of them, and saith unto them, Peace be unto you. But they were terrified and affrighted, and supposed that they had seen a spirit. And he said unto them, Why are ye troubled? and why do thoughts arise in your hearts? Behold my hands and my feet, that it is I myself; handle me and see, for a spirit hath not flesh and bones, as ye see me have.

And when he had thus spoken, he showed them his hands and his feet. And while they yet believed not for joy, and wondered, he said unto them, Have ye here any meat? And they gave him a piece of a broiled fish, and of an honeycomb. And he took it, and did eat before them. And he said unto them, These are the words which I spake unto you, while I was yet with you, that all things must be fulfilled which were written in the law of Moses, and in the prophets, and in the psalms, concerning me. Then opened he their understanding, that they might understand the scriptures, and said unto them, Thus it is written, and thus it behoved Christ to suffer, and to rise from the dead the third day: that repentance and remission of sins should be preached in his name among all nations, beginning at Jerusalem. And ye are witnesses of these things.

THEN the same day at evening, being the first of the week, when the doors were shut where the disciples were assembled for fear of the Jews, came Jesus and stood in the midst, and saith unto them, Peace be unto you. And as they sat at meat, he upbraided them with their unbelief, and hardness of heart, because they believed not them which had seen him after he was risen. And when he had so said, he showed unto them his hands and his side. Then were the disciples glad when they saw the Lord.

But Thomas, one of the twelve, called Didymus, was not with them when Jesus came. The other disciples therefore said unto him, We have seen the Lord. But he said unto them, Except I shall see in his hands the print of the nails, and put my finger into the print of the nails, and thrust my hand into his side, I will not believe. And after eight days again his disciples were within, and Thomas with them: then came Jesus, the doors being shut, and stood in the midst, and said, Peace be unto you. Then saith he to Thomas, Reach hither thy finger, and behold my hands; and reach hither thy hand, and thrust it into my side; and be not faithless, but believing. And

Thomas answered and said unto him, My Lord and my God! Jesus saith unto him, Thomas, because thou hast seen me, thou hast believed: blessed are they that have not seen' and yet have believed.

THEN the eleven disciples went away into Galilee, into a mountain where Jesus had appointed them. And when they saw him, they worshipped him: but some doubted. And Jesus came and spake unto them, saying, All power is given unto me in heaven and in earth: go ye, therefore, and teach all nations, baptizing them in the name of the Father, and of the Son, and of the Holy Ghost: teaching them to observe all things whatsoever I have commanded you: and, lo, I am with you alway, even unto the end of the world.

After these things Jesus showed himself again to the disciples at the sea of Tiberias, to whom also he showed himself alive after his passion by many infallible proofs, being seen of them forty days, and speaking of the things pertaining to the kingdom of God.

And from Jerusalem he led them out as far as to Bethany. And he said unto them, Ye shall receive power, after that the Holy Ghost is come upon you: and ye shall be witnesses unto me both in Jerusalem, and in all Judea, and in Samaria, and unto the uttermost part of the earth. And when he had spoken these things, while they beheld, he lifted up his hands, and blessed them. And it came to pass, while he blessed them, he was parted from them, received up into heaven, and sat on the right hand of God.

AND they went forth, and preached every where, the Lord working with them, and confirming the word with signs following. And with great power gave the apostles witness of the resurrection of the Lord Jesus, how that Christ died for our sins, according to the scriptures; that he was buried, and that he rose again the third day, according to the scriptures; and that he was seen of Cephas, then of the twelve; after that of above five hundred brethren at once; after that, of James; then of all the Apostles; and last of all of Paul also, as of one born out of due time.

THIS Jesus hath God raised up, whereof we all are witnesses.

FRUITAGE.

And as they spake unto the people, the priests, and the captain of the temple and the Sadducees, came upon them, being grieved that they taught the people, and preached through Jesus the resurrection from the dead: witnessing both to small and great, saying none other things than those which the prophets and Moses did say should come: that Christ should suffer, that he should be the first that should rise from the dead, and should show light unto the people, and to the Gentiles: and that he died for all, that they which live should not henceforth live unto themselves, but unto him which died for them, and rose again. The word which God sent, preaching peace: how God anointed Jesus of Nazareth with the Holy Ghost and with power; who went about doing good, and healing all that were oppressed of the devil; whom they slew and hanged on a tree: him God raised up the third day, and showed him openly; not to all the people, but unto witnesses chosen before of God, who did eat and drink with him after he rose from the dead, ordained of God to be the Judge of quick and dead. For to this end Christ both died, and rose, and revived, that he might be Lord both of the dead and living.

To him give all the prophets witness, that through his name whosoever believeth in him shall receive remission of sins. And the times of ignorance God winked at; but now commandeth all men every where to repent; because he hath appointed a day, in the which he will judge the world in righteousness, by that man whom he hath ordained; whereof he hath given assurance unto all men, in that he hath raised him from the dead; his Son Jesus Christ our Lord, which was made of the seed of David according to the flesh; and declared to be the Son of God with power by the resurrection from the dead: who verily was foreordained before the foundation of the world, but was manifest in these last times for you, who by him do believe in God, that raised him up from the dead, and gave him glory; him hath God exalted to be a Prince and a Saviour, to give repentance to Israel, and forgiveness of sins. For though he was crucified through weakness, yet he liveth by the power of God. And we also shall live with him by the power of God, if we believe on him that raised up Jesus our Lord from the dead; who was delivered for our offences, and was raised again for our justification.

FOR Christ also hath once suffered for sins, the Just for the unjust, that he might bring us to God, being put to death in the flesh, but quickened by the Spirit: but if the Spirit of him that raised up Jesus from the dead dwell in you, he that raised up Christ from the dead shall also quicken your mortal bodies by his Spirit that dwelleth in you. We had the sentence of death in ourselves, that we should not trust in ourselves, but in God, which raiseth the dead: and have hope toward God, that there shall be a resurrection of the dead, both of the just and unjust.

Knowing that he which raised up the Lord Jesus, shall raise up us also by Jesus, we faint not: for God hath not appointed us to wrath, but to obtain salvation by our Lord Jesus Christ, who died for us, that, whether we wake or sleep, we should live together with him: that like as he was raised up from the dead by the glory of the Father, even so we also should walk in newness of life. For if we have been planted together in the likeness of his death, we shall be also in the likeness of his resurrection. Now if we be dead with Christ, we believe that we shall also live with him: knowing that Christ, being raised from the dead, dieth no more; death hath no more dominion over him. Likewise reckon ye also yourselves to be dead indeed unto sin, but alive unto God through Jesus Christ our Lord.

Let this mind be in you, which was also in Christ Jesus: who, being in the form of God, thought it not robbery to be equal with God: but made himself of no reputation, and took upon him the form of a servant, and was made in the likeness of men: and being found in fashion as a man, he humbled himself, and became obedient unto death, even the death of the cross. Wherefore God also hath highly exalted him, and given him a name which is above every name: that at the name of Jesus every knee should bow, of things in heaven, and in earth, and under the earth; and that every tongue should confess that Jesus Christ is Lord, to the glory of God the Father.

Wherefore gird up the loins of your mind, be sober, and hope to the end for the grace that is to be brought unto you at the revelation of Jesus Christ: that ye may know what is the hope of his calling, and what the riches of the glory of his inheritance in the saints, and what is the exceeding greatness of his power to us-ward who believe, according to the working of his mighty power, which he wrought in Christ, when he raised him from the dead, and set him at his own right hand in the heavenly places, far above all principality, and power, and might, and dominion, and' every name that is named, not only in this world, but also in that which is to come. God hath both raised up the Lord, and will also raise up us by his own power. Why should it be thought a thing incredible with you, that God should raise the dead? And Jesus said, This is the Father's will which hath sent me, that of all which he hath given me I should lose nothing, but should raise it up at the last day. No man can come to me, except the Father which hath sent me draw him: and I will raise him up at the last day. For as the Father raiseth up the dead, and quickeneth them, even so the Son quickeneth whom he will. Marvel not at this: for the hour is coming, in the which all that are in the graves shall hear his voice, and shall come forth; they that have done good unto the resurrection of life, and they that have done evil unto the resurrection of damnation. For we must all appear before the judgment-seat of Christ; that every one may receive the things done in his body, according to that he hath done, whether it be good or bad. Verily, verily, I say unto you, He that heareth my word, and believeth on him that sent me, hath everlasting life, and shall not come into condemnation; but is passed from death unto life.

This is the will of him that sent me, that every one which seeth the Son, and believeth on him, may have everlasting life: and I will raise him up at the last day. Because I live, ye shall live also. Fear not; I am the first and the last: he that liveth, and was dead; and, behold, I am alive for evermore. I am the resurrection, and the life: he that believeth in me, though he were dead, yet shall he live. Blessed and holy is he that hath part in the first resurrection: on such the second death hath no power, but they shall be priests of God and of Christ, and shall reign with him a thousand years.

I count all things but loss that I may win Christ and be found in him; that I may know him, and the power of his resurrection, and the fellowship of his sufferings, being made conformable unto his death; if by any means I might attain unto the resurrection of the dead.

TRIUMPHS.

Blessed be the God and Father of our Lord Jesus Christ, which, according to his abundant mercy, hath begotten us again unto a lively hope by the resurrection of Jesus Christ from the dead, to an inheritance incorruptible, and undefiled, and that fadeth not away, reserved in heaven for you who are kept by the power of God through faith unto a salvation ready to be revealed in the last time, when he shall come to be glorified in his saints, and to be admired in all them that believe.

Now if Christ be preached that he rose from the dead, how say some among you that there is no resurrection of the dead? For if the dead rise not, then is not Christ raised. But now is Christ risen from the dead, and become the firstfruits of them that slept. For as in Adam all die, even so in Christ shall all be made alive. But every man in his own order: Christ the firstfruits; afterward they that are Christ's at his coming.

But some man will say, How are the dead raised up? and with what body do they come? Thou fool, that which thou sowest is not quickened, except it die: and that which thou sowest, thou sowest not that body that shall be, but bare grain, it may chance of wheat, or of some other grain: but God giveth it a body as it hath pleased him, and to every seed his own body. All flesh is not the same flesh: but there is one flesh of men, another flesh of beasts, another of fishes, and another of birds. There are also celestial bodies, and bodies terrestrial: but the glory of the celestial is one, and the glory of the terrestrial is another. There is one glory of the sun, and another glory of the moon, and another glory of the stars: for star differeth from star in glory. So also is the resurrection of the dead. It is sown in corruption, it is raised in incorruption: it is sown in dishonor, it is raised in glory: it is sown in weakness, it is raised in power: it is sown a natural body, it is raised a spiritual body. There is a natural body, and there is a spiritual body. Howbeit that was not first which is spiritual, but that which is natural; and afterward that which is spiritual. The first man is of the earth, earthy: the second man is the Lord from heaven. As is the earthy, such are they also that are earthy: and as is the heavenly, such are they also that are heavenly. And as we have borne the image of the earthy, we shall also bear the image of the heavenly.

Now this I say, brethren, that flesh and blood cannot inherit the kingdom of God, neither doth corruption inherit incorruption. Behold, I show you a mystery: we shall not all sleep, but we shall all be changed—in a moment, in the twinkling of an eye, at the last trump: for the trumpet shall sound, and the dead shall be raised incorruptible, and we shall be changed. For this corruptible must put on incorruption, and this mortal must put on immortality.

So when this corruptible shall have put on incorruption, and this mortal shall have put on immortality, then shall be brought to pass the saying that is written, Death is swallowed up in victory. O death, where is thy sting? O grave, where is thy victory? The sting of death is sin; and the strength of sin is the law. But thanks be to God, which giveth us the victory through our Lord Jesus Christ.

Therefore, my beloved brethren, be ye steadfast, unmovable, always abounding in the work of the Lord, forasmuch as ye know that your labor is not in vain in the Lord. For our conversation is in heaven; from whence also we look for the Saviour, the Lord Jesus Christ, who shall change our vile body, that it may be fashioned like unto his glorious body, according to the working whereby he is able even to subdue all things unto himself. For we know that if our earthly house of this tabernacle were dissolved, we have a building of God, an house not made with hands, eternal in the heavens. For in this we groan, earnestly desiring to be clothed upon with our house which is from heaven, that mortality might be swallowed up of life.

BUT I would not have you to be ignorant, brethren, concerning them which are asleep, that ye sorrow not, even as others which have no hope. For if we believe that Jesus died and rose again, even so them also which sleep in Jesus will God bring with him. For this we say unto you by the word of the Lord, that we which are alive and remain unto the coming of the Lord shall not go before them which are asleep. For the Lord himself shall descend from heaven with a shout, with the voice of the archangel, and with the trump of God: and the dead in Christ shall rise first; then we which are alive and remain shall be caught up together with them in the clouds to meet the Lord in the air: and so shall we ever be with the Lord.

AND he that sat upon the throne said, Behold, I make all things new. There shall be no more death, neither sorrow, nor crying, neither shall there be any more pain: for the former things are passed away. He that overcometh shall inherit all things; and I will be his God, and he shall be my son.

Without controversy, great is the mystery of godliness: He who was manifest in the flesh, justified in the Spirit, seen of angels, preached unto the Gentiles, believed on in the world, received up into glory.

GRACE be unto you, and peace, from him which is, and which was, and which is to come; and from the seven Spirits which are before his throne; and from Jesus Christ, who is the faithful witness, the first-begotten of the dead, and the prince of the kings of the earth.

UNTO him that loved us, and washed us from our sins in his own blood, and hath made us kings and priests unto

God and his Father; to him be glory and dominion for ever and ever. Amen.

Now the God of peace, that brought again from the dead our Lord Jesus, that great Shepherd of the sheep, through the blood of the everlasting covenant, make you perfect in every good work to do his will, working in you that which is well pleasing in his sight, through Jesus Christ; to whom be glory for ever and ever. Amen.

Scriptures for Affliction.

THE Lord gave, and the Lord hath taken away; blessed be the name of the Lord.

DARK QUESTIONINGS.

MAN that is born of a woman is of few days, and full of trouble. He cometh forth like a flower, and is cut down: he fleeth also as a shadow, and continueth not.

But Job answered and said, Have pity upon me, have pity upon me, O ye my friends; for the hand of God hath touched me. Oh that my grief were thoroughly weighed, and my calamity laid in the balances together! For the arrows of the Almighty are within me, the poison whereof drinketh up my spirit: so that my soul chooseth strangling, and death rather than my life. I loathe it; I would not live alway: let me alone; for my days are vanity.

1

My days are swifter than a weaver's shuttle, and are spent without hope, for now shall I sleep in the dust; and thou shalt seek me in the morning, but I shall not be. What is my strength, that I should hope? And what is mine end, that I should prolong my life? Oh that God would grant me the thing that I long for! that he would let loose his hand, and cut me off! Wherefore is light given to him that is in misery, and life unto the bitter in soul; which long for death, but it cometh not; and are glad when they can find the grave?

If a man die, shall he live again? There is hope of a tree, if it be cut down, that it will sprout again; but man dieth, and wasteth away: yea, man giveth up the ghost, and where is he? As the cloud is consumed and vanisheth away, so he that goeth down to the grave shall come up no more. Man lieth down, and riseth not: till the heavens be no more, they shall not awake, nor be raised out of their sleep. O that thou wouldest hide me in the grave, that thou wouldest keep me secret, until thy wrath be past.

Let me alone, that I may take comfort a little, before I go whence I shall not return; to the land of the shadow of death, without any order, and where the light is as darkness. There the wicked cease from troubling, and there the weary be at rest. There the prisoners rest together; they hear not the voice of the oppressor. The small and great are there; and the servant is free from his master.

CRIES OF SUFFERING.

Although affliction cometh not forth of the dust, neither doth trouble spring out of the ground; yet man is born unto trouble, as the sparks fly upward. I would seek unto God, and unto God would I commit my cause.

I have sinned; what shall I do unto thee, O thou preserver of men? Why hast thou set me as a mark against thee, so that I am a burden to myself? And why dost thou not pardon my transgression, and take away mine iniquity?

Out of the depths have I cried unto thee, O Lord. Turn thee unto me, and have mercy upon me; for I am desolate and afflicted. The troubles of my heart are enlarged: O bring thou me out of my distresses. Look upon mine affliction and my pain, and forgive all my sins.

I cried by reason of mine affliction unto the Lord, and he heard me. I said, I am cast out of thy sight; my strength and my hope is perished from the Lord. Is it nothing to you, all ye that pass by? Behold, and see if there be any sorrow like unto my sorrow, which is done unto me, wherewith the Lord hath afflicted me in the day of his fierce anger. He hath bent his bow, and set me as a mark for the arrow. For these things I weep; mine eye, mine eye runneth down with water, because the comforter that should relieve my soul is far from me.

O my God, my soul is cast down within me: all thy waves and thy billows are gone over me. Will the

Lord cast off forever? and will he be favorable no more? Is his mercy clean gone forever? doth his promise fail for evermore? Hath God forgotten to be gracious? Hath he in anger shut up his tender mercies?

O my God, I cry in the day-time, but thou hearest not; and in the night season, and am not silent. But thou art holy, O thou that inhabitest the praises of Israel. Turn thee unto me, and have mercy upon me; for I am desolate and afflicted. Look upon mine affliction and my pain; and forgive all my sins.

When my soul fainted within me I remembered the Lord, and my prayer came in unto thee, into thine holy temple.

Wherefore doth a living man complain, a man for the punishment of his sins? If thou, Lord, shouldest mark iniquities, O Lord, who shall stand? But there is forgiveness with thee, that thou mayest be feared.

Remember, O Lord, thy tender mercies and thy loving-kindnesses; for they have been ever of old. Remember not the sins of my youth, nor my transgressions: according to thy mercy remember thou me for thy goodness' sake, O Lord. O keep my soul, and deliver me: let me not be ashamed; for I put my trust in thee.

HEAR, O Lord, when I cry with my voice: have mercy also upon me, and answer me. When thou saidst, Seek ye my face; my heart said unto thee, Thy face, Lord, will I seek. Hide not thy face far from me; put not thy servant away in anger: thou hast been my help; leave me not, neither forsake me, O God of my salvation.

When my father and my mother forsake me, then the Lord will take me up: for he hath said, I will never leave . thee, nor forsake thee.

For a small moment have I forsaken thee; but with great mercies will I gather thee. In a little wrath I hid my face from thee for a moment; but with everlasting kindness will I have mercy on thee, saith the Lord thy Redeemer.

For thy Maker is thine husband; the Lord of hosts is his name; and thy

Redeemer the Holy One of Israel: the mountains shall depart, and the hills be removed; but my kindness shall not depart from thee, neither shall the covenant of my peace be removed, saith the Lord that hath mercy on thee.

PRAYERS OF WEAKNESS.

Remember how short my time is: wherefore hast thou made all men in vain? What man is he that liveth, and shall not see death? shall he deliver his soul from the hand of the grave? There is no man that hath power over the spirit to retain the spirit: neither hath he power in the day of death. For all flesh is as grass, and all the glory of man as the flower of grass, because as the flower of the grass he shall pass away. For the sun is no sooner risen with a burning heat, but it withereth the grass, and the flower thereof falleth, and the grace of the fashion of it perisheth.

LORD, make me to know mine end and the measure of my days, what it is; that I may know how frail I am. Behold, thou hast made my days as a hand-breath, and mine age is as nothing before thee: verily every man at his best state is altogether vanity. Surely every man walketh in a vain show: surely they are disquieted in vain; he heapeth up riches, and knoweth not who shall gather them.

And now, Lord, what wait I for? my hope is in thee. They that trust in their wealth, and boast themselves in the multitude of their riches, none of them can by any means redeem his brother, nor give to God a ransom for him; that he should still live for ever, and not see corruption. For, when he dieth, he shall carry nothing away; like sheep they are laid in the grave; death shall feed on them.

But God will redeem my soul from the power of the grave; for he shall receive me. Hear my prayer, O Lord, and give ear unto my cry; hold not thy peace at my tears; for I am a stranger with thee, and a sojourner, as all my fathers were.

LORD, thou hast been our dwelling place in all generations. Before the mountains were brought forth, or ever thou hadst formed the earth and the world, even from everlasting to everlasting, thou art God.

Thou turnest man to destruction; and sayest, Return, ye children of men. For a thousand years in thy sight are but as yesterday when it is past, and as a watch in the night.

Thou carriest them away as with a flood; they are as a sleep: in the morning they are like grass which groweth up. In the morning it flourisheth, and groweth up; in the evening it is cut down, and withereth. For we are consumed by thine anger, and by thy wrath are we troubled. Thou hast set our iniquities before thee, our secret sins in the light of thy countenance. For all our days are passed away in thy wrath; we spend our years as a tale that is told.

The days of our years are three-score years and ten; and if by reason of strength they be fourscore years, yet is their strength labor and sorrow: for it is soon cut off, and we fly away.

So teach us to number our days that we may apply our hearts unto wisdom. O satisfy us early with thy mercy; that we may rejoice and be glad all our days. Make us glad according to the days wherein thou hast afflicted us, and the years wherein we have seen evil.

SONGS OF TRUST.

Bless the Lord, O my soul; and all that is within me, bless his holy name. Bless the Lord, O my soul, and forget not all his benefits: who forgiveth all thine iniquities; who healeth all thy diseases; who redeemeth thy life from destruction; who crowneth thee with loving-kindness and tender mercies.

The Lord is merciful and gracious, slow to anger, and plenteous in mercy. He will not always chide; neither will he keep his anger for ever. He hath not dealt with us after our sins, nor rewarded us according to our iniquities.

For as the heaven is high above the earth, so great is his mercy toward them that fear him. As far as the east is from the west, so far hath he removed our trangressions from us.

Like as a father pitieth his children, so the Lord pitieth them that fear him. For he knoweth our frame; he remembereth that we are dust.

As for man, his days are as grass: as a flower of the field so he flourisheth: for the wind passeth over it, and it is gone; and the place thereof shall know it no more.

But the mercy of the Lord is from everlasting to everlasting upon them that fear him, and his righteousness unto children's children; to such as keep his covenant, and to those that remember his commandments to do them.

THE LORD is gracious, and full of compassion; slow to anger, and of great mercy. The Lord is good to all, and his tender mercies are over all his works. He will fulfill the desire of them that fear him; he also will hear their cry, and will save them. For he said, Surely they are my people. In all their affliction he was afflicted, and the angel of his presence saved them: in his love and in his pity he redeemed them; and he bare them, and carried them all the days of old.

The Lord will command his loving kindness in the day-time, and in the night his song shall be with me, and my prayer unto the God of my life. He healeth the broken in heart, and bindeth up their wounds. I was brought low, and he helped me.

Return unto thy rest, O my soul; for the Lord hath dealt bountifully with thee. Thou hast delivered my soul from death, mine eyes from tears, and my feet from falling. I will walk before the Lord in the land of the living.

O, taste and see that the Lord is good: blessed is the man that trusteth in him.

Why art thou cast down, O my soul? and why art thou disquieted within me? Hope thou in God: for I shall yet praise him, who is the health of my countenance and my God.

THE righteous cry, and the Lord heareth, and delivereth them out of all their troubles. The Lord is nigh unto them that are of a broken heart, and saveth such as be of a contrite spirit. Many are the afflictions of the righteous: but the Lord delivereth him out of them all.

Preserve me, O God, for in thee do I put my trust. Precious in the sight of the Lord is the death of his saints. Though he slay me, yet will I trust in him. My flesh also shall rest in hope. I know that it shall be well with them that fear God.

Mark the perfect man, and behold the upright: for the end of that man is peace.

Thou wilt show me the path of life: in thy presence is fullness of joy; at thy right hand there are pleasures for evermore.

BLESSINGS IN TRIALS.

Comfort ye, comfort ye my people, saith your God. All flesh is grass, and all the goodliness thereof is as the flower of the field: the grass withereth, the flower fadeth; but the word of our God shall stand for ever.

BEHOLD, happy is the man whom God correcteth: therefore despise not thou the chastening of the Almighty. Though he cause grief, yet will he have compassion according to the multitude of his mercies. For he doth not afflict willingly, nor grieve the children of men.

My son, despise not thou the chastening of the Lord, nor faint when thou art rebuked of him: for whom the Lord loveth he chasteneth, and scourgeth every son whom he receiveth. If ye endure chastening, God dealeth with you as with sons; for what son is he whom the father chasteneth not? No chastening for the present seemeth to be joyous, but grievous: nevertheless, afterward it yieldeth the peaceable fruit of righteousness unto them which are exercised thereby.

It is good for me that I have been afflicted; that I might learn thy statutes.   Before I was afflicted I went astray; but now have I kept thy word. It is good that a man should both hope and quietly wait for the salvation of the Lord.

BLESSED is the man that endureth temptation: for when he is tried, he shall receive the crown of life, which the Lord hath promised to them that love him: wherein ye greatly rejoice, though now for a season ye are in heaviness through manifold temptations: that the trial of your faith, being much more precious than of gold that perisheth, though it be tried with fire, might be found unto praise and honor and glory at the appearing of Jesus Christ: whom having not seen, ye love; in whom, though now ye see him not, yet believing, ye rejoice with joy unspeakable and full of glory: receiving the end of your faith, even the salvation of your souls.   For which cause we faint not; but though our outward man perish, yet the inward man is renewed day by day.

For our light affliction, which is but for a moment, worketh for us a far more exceeding and eternal weight of glory. While we look not at the things which are seen, but at the things which are not seen: for the things which are seen are temporal; but the things which are not seen are eternal.

But the God of all grace, who hath called us unto his eternal glory by Christ Jesus, after that ye have suffered a while, make you perfect, stablish, strengthen, settle you. To him be glory and dominion for ever and ever. Amen.

GOD'S COMFORTS.

Grace be to you and peace from God our Father, and from the Lord Jesus Christ. Blessed be God, even the Father of our Lord Jesus Christ, the Father of mercies, and the God of all comfort; who comforteth us in all our tribulation, that we may be able to comfort them which are in any trouble by the comfort wherewith we ourselves are comforted of God.

For as the sufferings of Christ abound in us, so our consolation also aboundeth by Christ.

HE shall feed his flock like a shepherd: he shall gather the lambs with his arm, and carry them in his bosom, and shall gently lead those that are with young.

AND they brought young children to him, that he should touch them: and his disciples rebuked those that brought them. But when Jesus saw it, he was much displeased, and said unto them, Suffer the little children to come unto me, and forbid them not: for of such is the kingdom of God. Verily I say unto you, Whosoever shall not receive the kingdom of God as a little child, he shall not enter therein.

Take heed that ye despise not one of these little ones; for I say unto you, that in heaven their angels do always behold the face of my Father which is in heaven. For the Son of man is come to save that which was lost. Even so, it is not the will of your Father which is in heaven that one of these little ones should perish. And he took them up in his arms, put his hands upon them, and blessed them.

AND Jesus called a little child unto him and set him in the midst of them, and said, Verily, I say unto you, except ye be converted, and become as little children, ye shall not enter into the kingdom of heaven. Whosoever therefore shall humble himself as this little child, the same is greatest in the kingdom of heaven. And whoso shall receive one such little child in my name, receiveth me.

AND the Lord struck the child that Uriah's wife bare unto David, and it was very sick. David therefore besought God for the child; and David fasted, and went in and lay all night upon the earth. And it came to pass on the seventh day that the child died. And the servants of David feared to tell him that the child was dead: for they said, Behold, while the child was yet alive we spake unto him, and he would not hearken unto our voice; how will he then vex himself if we tell him that the child is dead!

But when David saw that his servants whispered, David perceived that the child was dead: therefore David said unto his servants, Is the child dead? And they said, He is dead. Then David arose from the earth, and washed, and anointed himself, and changed his apparel, and came into the house of the Lord, and worshipped: then he came to his own house; and when he required, they set bread before him, and he did eat.

Then said his servants unto him, What thing is this that thou hast done? Thou didst fast and weep for the child while it was alive; but when the child was dead, thou didst rise and eat bread.

And he said, While the child was yet alive, I fasted and wept: for I said, Who can tell whether God will be gracious to me, that the child may live? But now he is dead, wherefore should I fast? can I bring him back again? I shall go to him, but he shall not return to me.

NOW a certain man was sick, named Lazarus, of Bethany. Therefore his sisters sent unto Jesus, saying, Lord, behold, he whom thou lovest is sick. Now Jesus loved Martha, and her sister, and Lazarus. When he had heard therefore that he was sick, he abode two days still in the same place where he was. Then after that saith he to his disciples, Let us go into Judea again. Our friend Lazarus sleepeth; but I go that I may awake him out of sleep. Then said his disciples, Lord, if he sleep, he shall do well. Then said Jesus unto them plainly, Lazarus is dead. And I am glad for your sakes that I was not there, to the intent ye may believe; nevertheless, let us go unto him. Then when Jesus came, he found that he had lain in the grave four days already. Then said Martha unto Jesus, Lord, if thou hadst been here, my brother had not died. But I know, that even now, whatsoever thou wilt ask of God, God will give it thee. Jesus saith unto her, Thy brother shall rise again. Martha saith unto him, I know that he shall rise again in the resurrection at the last day.

Jesus said unto her, I am the resurrection, and the life: he that believeth in me, though he were dead, yet shall he live. And whosoever liveth and believeth in me shall never die.

THEN said Jesus unto them again, I lay down my life for the sheep. No man taketh it from me, but I lay it down of myself. I have power to lay it down, and I have power to take it again. My sheep hear my voice, and I know them, and they follow me: and I give unto them eternal life; and they shall never perish, neither shall any man pluck them out of my hand. My Father, which gave them me, is greater than all; and no man is able to pluck them out of my Father's hand. And this is the Father's will which hath sent me, that of all which he hath given me, I should lose nothing, but should raise it up again at the last day.

Blessed be the God and Father of our Lord Jesus Christ, which according to his abundant mercy hath begotten us again unto a lively hope by the resurrection of Jesus Christ from the dead, to an inheritance incorruptible, and undefiled, and that fadeth not away, reserved in heaven for you, who are kept by the power of God through faith unto salvation, ready to be re-vealed in the last time: troubled on every side, yet not distressed; per-plexed, but not in despair; persecuted, but not forsaken; cast down, but not destroyed; always bearing about in the body the dying of the Lord Jesus, that the life also of Jesus might be made manifest in our mortal flesh.

Knowing, that he which raised up the Lord Jesus, shall raise up us also by Jesus, we faint not; but though our outward man perish, yet the inward man is renewed day by day. And our hope of you is steadfast, knowing, that as ye are partakers of the sufferings, so shall ye be also of the consolation.

Eye hath not seen, nor ear heard, neither have entered into the heart of man, the things which God hath prepared for them that love him; but God hath revealed them unto us by his Spirit.

THERE remaineth therefore a rest to the people of God. Come unto me, all ye that labor and are heavy laden, and I will give you rest. Take my yoke upon you, and learn of me: for I am meek and lowly in heart; and ye shall find rest unto your souls.

EXAMPLES OF PATIENCE.

Take, my brethren, the prophets, who have spoken in the name of the Lord, for an example of suffering affliction, and of patience. Behold, we count them happy which endure. Ye have heard of the patience of Job, and have seen the end of the Lord; that the Lord is very pitiful, and of tender mercy.

By faith Abraham, when he was called to go out into a place which he should after receive for an inheritance, obeyed; and he went out, not knowing whither he went. By faith he sojourned in the land of promise, as in a strange country, dwelling in tabernacles with Isaac and Jacob, the heirs with him of the same promise: for he looked for a city which hath foundations, whose builder and maker is God.

These all died in faith, not having received the promises, but having seen them afar off, and were persuaded of them, and embraced them, and confessed that they were strangers and pilgrims on the earth. For they that say such things declare plainly that they seek a country. And truly, if they had been mindful of that country from whence they came out, they might have had opportunity to have returned. But now they desire a better country, that is, an heavenly: wherefore God is not ashamed to be called their God; for he hath prepared for them a city.

By faith Moses, when he was come to years, refused to be called the son of Pharaoh's daughter; choosing rather to suffer affliction with the people of God, than to enjoy the pleasures of sin for a season; esteeming the reproach of Christ greater riches than the treasures in Egypt: for he had respect unto the recompense of the reward. By faith he forsook Egypt, not fearing the wrath of the king: for he endured, as seeing Him who is invisible.

Women received their dead raised to life again: and others were tortured, not accepting deliverance; that they might obtain a better resurrection.

And others had trial of cruel mockings and scourgings, yea, moreover of bonds and imprisonment. They were stoned, they were sawn asunder, were tempted, were slain with the sword: they wandered about in sheepskins and goatskins; being destitute, afflicted, tormented; (of whom the world was not worthy:) they wandered in deserts, and in mountains, and in dens and caves of the earth. And these all, having obtained a good report through faith, received not the promise: God having provided some better thing for us, that they without us should not be made perfect.

OUR SUPREME EXAMPLE.

Wherefore, holy brethren, partakers of the heavenly calling, consider the Apostle and High Priest of our profession, Christ Jesus, who, in the days of his flesh, when he had offered up prayers and supplications with strong crying and tears unto him that was able to save him from death, and was heard in that he feared: though he were a Son, yet learned he obedience by the things which he suffered. He was oppressed, and he was afflicted; he is brought as a lamb to the slaughter; and as a sheep before her shearers is dumb, so he openeth not his mouth. He is despised and rejected of men; a man of sorrows, and acquainted with grief. Surely he hath borne our griefs, and carried our sorrows: yet we did esteem him stricken, smitten of God, and afflicted. It pleased the Lord to bruise him; he hath put him to grief; for it became him, for whom are all things, and by whom are all things, in bringing many sons unto glory, to make the captain of their salvation perfect through sufferings.

And being made perfect, he became the author of eternal salvation unto all them that obey him: for which cause he is not ashamed to call them brethren. Wherefore in all things it behooved him to be made like unto his brethren, that he might be a merciful and faithful high priest in things pertaining to God, to make reconciliation for the sins of the people. For in that he himself hath suffered being tempted, he is able to succor them that are tempted.

Forasmuch then as the children are partakers of flesh and blood, he also himself likewise took part of the same; that through death he might destroy him that had the power of death, that is, the devil; and deliver them, who through fear of death were all their lifetime subject to bondage.

Seeing then that we have a great high priest, that is passed into the heavens, Jesus the Son of God: not a high priest which cannot be touched with the feeling of our infirmities, but was in all points tempted like as we are, yet without sin: let us come boldly unto the throne of grace, that we may obtain mercy, and find grace to help in time of need. Let us go forth unto him without the camp, bearing his reproach. For here we have no continuing city, but we seek one to come.

And there were certain Greeks among them that came up to worship at the feast. The same came therefore to Philip, which was of Bethsaida of Galilee, and desired him, saying, Sir, we would see Jesus. Philip cometh and telleth Andrew: and again, Andrew and Philip tell Jesus.

And Jesus answered, saying, The hour is come, that the Son of man should be glorified. Except a corn of wheat fall into the ground and die, it abideth alone: but if it die, it bringeth forth much fruit. Herein is my Father glorified, that ye bear much fruit. Ye have not chosen me, but I have chosen you, and ordained you, that ye should go and bring forth fruit, and that your fruit should remain. Every branch in me that beareth not fruit he taketh away: and every branch that beareth fruit, he purgeth it, that it may bring forth more fruit. He that loveth father or mother more than me, is not worthy of me; and he that loveth son or daughter more than me, is not worthy of me; and he that taketh not his cross, and followeth after me, is not worthy of me. If any man serve me, let him follow me; and where I am, there shall also my servant be. It is enough for the disciple that he be as his master, and the servant as his lord. If the world hate you, ye know that it hated me before it hated you. If ye were of the world, the world would love his own; but because ye are not of the world, but I have chosen you out of the world, therefore the world hateth you. Remember the word that I said unto you—The servant is not greater than his lord. If they have persecuted me, they will also persecute you. But all these things will they do unto you for my name's sake; ye shall weep and lament, but the world shall rejoice; and ye shall be sorrowful, but your sorrow shall be turned into joy. I will see you again, and your heart shall rejoice, and your joy no man taketh from you.

Now is my soul troubled; and what shall I say? Father, save me from this hour: but for this cause came I unto this hour. Father, glorify thy name.

THEN cometh Jesus with the disciples unto a place called Gethsemane. And he took with him Peter and the two sons of Zebedee, and saith unto them, My soul is exceeding sorrowful, even unto death: tarry ye here, and watch with me.

And he went a little farther, and fell on his face, and prayed, saying, O my Father, if it be possible, let this cup pass from me: nevertheless, not as I will, but as thou wilt. And there appeared an angel unto him from heaven, strengthening him. And being in an agony, he prayed more earnestly: and his sweat was as it were great drops of blood falling down to the ground. And he cometh unto the disciples and findeth them asleep, and saith unto Peter, What, could ye not watch with me one hour? He went away again the second time, and prayed, saying, O my Father, if this cup may not pass away from me, except I drink it, thy will be done. And he came and found them asleep again: for their eyes were heavy. And he left them, and went away again, and prayed the third time, saying the same words.

Then cometh he to his disciples, and saith unto them, Sleep on now; behold, the hour is at hand, and the Son of man is betrayed into the hands of sinners: the cup which my Father hath given me, shall I not drink it? Rise, let us be going: behold, he is at hand that doth betray me. And while he yet spake, lo, Judas, one of the twelve, came, and with him a great multitude with swords and staves,

31

from the chief priests and elders of the people.

AND they that had laid hold on Jesus led him away to Caiaphas the high priest, where the chief priests, and elders, and all the council, sought false witness against Jesus, to put him to death. But Jesus held his peace. And the high priest answered and said unto him, I adjure thee by the living God, that thou tell us whether thou be the Christ, the Son of God. Jesus saith unto him, Thou hast said: nevertheless, I say unto you, hereafter shall ye see the Son of man sitting on the right hand of the power of God, and coming in the clouds of heaven. Then said they all, Art thou then the Son of God? And he said unto them, Ye say that I am. And they said, What need we any further witness? for we ourselves have heard of his own mouth. He hath spoken blasphemy; he is guilty of death. Then did they spit in his face, and buffeted him; and others smote him with the palms of their hands.

And the whole multitude of them arose, and bound Jesus and carried him away, and delivered him to Pilate, saying, We found this fellow perverting the nation, and forbidding to give tribute to Cæsar, saying, that he himself is Christ, a King. And Pilate asked him, saying, Art thou the King of the Jews? And he answered him and said, Thou sayest. And Pilate said unto them, What will ye that I shall do unto him whom ye call the King of the Jews? And they cried out again, Crucify him! Then Pilate said unto them, Why, what evil hath he done? Ye have brought this man unto me, as one that perverteth the people: and behold, I, having examined him before you, have found no fault in this man, touching those things whereof ye accuse him; I will therefore chastise him, and release him.

THEN Pilate therefore took Jesus, and scourged him. Then the soldiers of the governor took Jesus into the common hall, and gathered unto him the whole band of soldiers. And they stripped him, and put on him a scarlet robe. And when they had platted a crown of thorns, they put it upon his head, and a reed in his right hand: and they bowed the knee before him, and mocked him, saying, Hail, King of the Jews! And they spit upon him, and took the reed, and smote him on the head.

Pilate therefore went forth again, and saith unto them, Behold, I bring him forth to you, that ye may know that I find no fault in him. Then came Jesus forth, wearing the crown of thorns and the purple robe. And Pilate saith unto them, Behold the man! When the chief priests therefore and officers saw him, they cried out, saying, Crucify, crucify him! Pilate saith unto them, Take ye him, and crucify him; for I find no fault in him. The Jews answered him, We have a law, and by our law he ought to die, because he made himself the Son of God. And from thenceforth Pilate sought to release him: but the Jews cried out, saying, If thou let this man go, thou art not Cæsar's friend:

whosoever maketh himself a king speaketh against Cæsar.

When Pilate therefore heard that saying, he brought Jesus forth, and sat down in the judgment seat in a place that is called the Pavement, and he saith unto the Jews, Behold your King! But they cried out, Away with him, away with him, crucify him! Pilate saith unto them, Shall I crucify your King? The chief priests answered, We have no king but Cæsar.

When Pilate saw that he could prevail nothing, but that rather a tumult was made, he took water, and washed his hands before the multitude, saying, I am innocent of the blood of this just person: see ye to it. Then answered all the people, and said, His blood be on us, and on our children. Then delivered he him therefore unto them to be crucified. And they took Jesus, and led him away. And there were also two others, malefactors, led with him to be put to death. And he, bearing his cross, went forth into a place which is called Calvary, where they crucified him, and the two malefactors with him, on either side one, and Jesus in the midst.

AND they that passed by reviled him, wagging their heads, and saying, Thou that destroyest the temple, and buildest it in three days, save thyself. If thou be the Son of God, come down from the cross.

Likewise also the chief priests mocking him, with the scribes and elders, said, He saved others; himself he cannot save. If he be the King of Israel, let him now come down from the cross, and we will believe him. He trusted in God; let him deliver him now, if he will have him: for he said, I am the Son of God.

The thieves also, which were crucified with him, cast the same in his teeth.

Then said Jesus, Father, forgive them; for they know not what they do.

And one of the malefactors which were hanged railed on him, saying, If thou be Christ, save thyself and us. But the other answering rebuked

him, saying, Dost not thou fear God,
seeing thou art in the same condemnation? And we indeed justly; for we
receive the due reward of our deeds:
but this man hath done nothing amiss.
And he said unto Jesus, Lord, remember me when thou comest into thy
kingdom. And Jesus said unto him,
Verily I say unto thee, to-day shalt
thou be with me in paradise.

Now there stood by the cross of
Jesus, his mother. When Jesus therefore saw his mother, and the disciple
standing by whom he loved, he saith
unto his mother, Woman, behold thy
son! Then saith he to the disciple,
Behold thy mother! And from that
hour that disciple took her unto his
own home.

And when the sixth hour was
come, there was darkness over the
whole land until the ninth hour.
Jesus knowing that all things were
now accomplished, that the scripture
might be fulfilled, saith, I thirst. Now
there was set a vessel full of vinegar:
and they filled a sponge with vinegar,
and put it upon hyssop, and put it to

his mouth. When Jesus therefore had received the vinegar, he said, It is finished.

And at the ninth hour Jesus cried with a loud voice, saying, Eloi, Eloi, lama sabachthani? which is, being interpreted, My God, my God, why hast thou forsaken me? And the sun was darkened, and the veil of the temple was rent in the midst; and the earth did quake, and the rocks rent; and the graves were opened; and many bodies of the saints which slept arose, and came out of the graves after his resurrection, and went into the holy city, and appeared unto many. And when Jesus had cried with a loud voice, he said, Father, into thy hands I commend my spirit: and having said thus, he gave up the ghost.

WHEN the centurion, and they that were with him, watching Jesus, saw the earthquake, and those things that were done, they feared greatly, saying, Truly this was the Son of God. But one of the soldiers with a spear pierced his side, and forthwith came there out blood and water. They shall look on him whom they pierced.

Now in the place where he was crucified there was a garden, and in the garden a new sepulchre, wherein was never man yet laid. When the even was come, Joseph of Arimathæa, an honorable counsellor, which also waited for the kingdom of God, came, and went in boldly unto Pilate, and craved the body of Jesus. And Pilate marvelled if he were already dead: and calling unto him the centurion, he asked him whether he had been any while dead. And when he knew it of the centurion, he gave the body to Joseph. And when Joseph had taken the body, he wrapped it in a clean linen cloth, and laid it in his own new tomb, which he had hewn out in the rock; and he rolled a great stone to the door of the sepulchre, and departed.

He was taken from prison and from judgment: for he was cut off out of the land of the living: for the transgression of my people was he stricken. And he made his grave with the wicked, and with the rich in his death; because he had done no violence, neither was any deceit in his mouth.

FORASMUCH then as Christ hath suffered for us in the flesh, arm yourselves likewise with the same mind: looking unto Jesus, the author and finisher of our faith; who for the joy that was set before him endured the cross, despising the shame, and is set down at the right hand of the throne of God.   For consider him that endured such contradiction of sinners against himself, lest ye be wearied and faint in your minds.   For even hereunto were ye called: because Christ also suffered for us, leaving an example, that ye should follow his steps.

Beloved, think it not strange, concerning the fiery trial which is to try you, as though some strange thing happened unto you: but rejoice, inasmuch as ye are partakers of Christ's sufferings; knowing that the same afflictions are accomplished in your brethren that are in the world.   For unto you it is given in the behalf of Christ, not only to believe on him, but also to suffer for his sake.

RECOMPENSE OF REWARD.

Wherefore, let them that suffer according to the will of God, commit the keeping of their souls to him in well-doing, as unto a faithful Creator, knowing that ye are thereunto called, that ye should inherit a blessing. For none of us liveth to himself, and no man dieth to himself. For whether we live, we live unto the Lord; and whether we die, we die unto the Lord; whether we live therefore, or die, we are the Lord's; as dying, and, behold, we live; as chastened, and not killed; as sorrowful, yet always rejoicing; as poor, yet making many rich; as having nothing, and yet possessing all things.

For if we would judge ourselves, we should not be judged. But when we are judged, we are chastened of the Lord, that we should not be condemned with the world: who will render to every man according to his deeds: to them who by patient continuance in well-doing, seek for glory, and honor, and immortality, eternal life: glory, honor, and peace, to every man that worketh good; to the Jew first, and also to the Gentile; for there is no respect of persons with God. Despisest thou the riches of his goodness, and forbearance, and long-suffering; not knowing that the goodness of God leadeth thee to repentance?

As many as I love, I rebuke and chasten: be zealous therefore, and repent. For ye were as sheep going astray; but are now returned unto the Shepherd and Bishop of your souls: and when the chief Shepherd shall appear, ye shall receive a crown of glory that fadeth not away.

KEEP yourselves in the love of God, looking for the mercy of our Lord Jesus Christ unto eternal life. For ye have not received the spirit of bondage again to fear; but ye have received the spirit of adoption, whereby we cry, Abba, Father. The Spirit itself beareth witness with our spirit, that we are the children of God: and if children, then heirs: heirs of God, and joint-heirs with Christ; if so be that we suffer with him, that we may be also glorified together. For I reckon that the sufferings of this present time are not worthy to be compared with the glory which shall be revealed in us. He that spared not his own Son, but delivered him up for us all, how shall he not with him also freely give us all things.

Who shall lay any thing to the charge of God's elect? It is God that justifieth. Who is he that condemneth? It is Christ that died, yea rather, that is risen again, who is even at the right hand of God, who also maketh intercession for us. Who shall separate us from the love of Christ? Shall tribulation, or distress, or persecution, or famine, or nakedness, or peril, or sword? Nay, in all these things we are more than conquerors, through him that loved us. For I am persuaded, that neither death, nor life, nor angels, nor principalities, nor powers, nor things present, nor things to come, nor height, nor depth, nor any other creature, shall be able to separate us from the love of God which is in Christ Jesus our Lord.

BE thou faithful unto death, and I will give thee a crown of life. He that loveth his life shall lose it; and he that hateth his life in this world, shall keep it unto life eternal.

NOW unto him that is able to keep you from falling, and to present you faultless before the presence of his glory with exceeding joy, to the only wise God our Saviour, be glory and majesty, dominion and power, both now and ever. Amen.

THE FUTURE SECURE IN OUR RISEN LORD.

Then said Jesus, Let not your heart be troubled: ye believe in God, believe also in me. In my Father's house are many mansions: if it were not so, I

would have told you. I go to prepare
a place for you. And if I go and
prepare a place for you, I will come
again, and receive you unto myself;
that where I am, there ye may be
also. I will not leave you comfortless;
I will come to you: because I live, ye
shall live also. And I will pray the
Father, and he shall give you another
Comforter, that he may abide with
you for ever; even the Spirit of truth;
whom the world cannot receive, because it seeth him not, neither knoweth him: but ye know him; for he
dwelleth with you, and shall be in
you. But the Comforter, which is the
Holy Ghost, whom the Father will
send in my name, he shall teach you
all things, and bring all things to your
remembrance, whatsoever I have said
unto you. Peace I leave with you,
my peace I give unto you; not as the
world giveth, give I unto you. Let
not your heart be troubled, neither let
it be afraid. These things I have
spoken unto you, that in me ye might
have peace. In the world ye shall
have tribulation: but be of good cheer;

I have overcome the world. To him that overcometh will I give to eat of the tree of life, which is in the midst of the paradise of God, and he shall go no more out: and I will write upon him the name of my God, and I will not blot out his name out of the book of life, but I will confess his name before my Father, and before his angels. Father, I will that they also whom thou hast given me be with me where I am.

I KNOW that my Redeemer liveth, and that he shall stand at the latter day upon the earth.

Him God raised up the third day, and showed him openly; not to all the people, but unto witnesses chosen before of God, who did eat and drink with him after he rose from the dead. To whom also he showed himself alive after his passion by many infallible proofs, being seen of them forty days, and speaking of the things pertaining to the kingdom of God.

And he said unto them, Thus it is written, and thus it behooved Christ to suffer, and to rise from the dead the third day. These are the words which I spake unto you, while I was yet with you, that all things must be fulfilled, which were written in the law of Moses, and in the prophets, and in the psalms, concerning me. Ought not Christ to have suffered these things, and to enter into his glory.

And he led them out as far as to Bethany, and he lifted up his hands and blessed them. And it came to pass while he blessed them, he was parted from them and carried up into heaven, and a cloud received him out of their sight. And while they looked steadfastly toward heaven as he went up, behold, two men stood by them in white apparel; which also said, Ye men of Galilee, why stand ye gazing up into heaven? This same Jesus which is taken up from you into heaven, shall so come in like manner as ye have seen him go into heaven.

I know whom I have believed, and am persuaded that he is able to keep that which I have committed unto him against that day. Who is gone

into heaven, and is on the right hand
of God; angels and authorities and
powers being made subject unto him.
Seek those things which are above,
where Christ sitteth on the right hand
of God. Set your affection on things
above, not on things on the earth:
confident that he which hath begun a
good work in you will perform it until
the day of Jesus Christ.

Beloved, now are we the sons of
God, and it doth not yet appear what
we shall be: but we know that, when
he shall appear, we shall be like him;
for we shall see him as he is. When
Christ, who is our life, shall appear,
then shall ye also appear with him in
glory. For our conversation is in
heaven; from whence also we look for
the Saviour, the Lord Jesus Christ;
who shall change our vile body, that
it may be fashioned like unto his
glorious body, according to the working whereby he is able even to subdue
all things unto himself.

For we know, that if our earthly
house of this tabernacle were dis-

solved, we have a building of God, a house not made with hands, eternal in the heavens. For in this we groan, earnestly desiring to be clothed upon with our house which is from heaven: if so be that being clothed we shall not be found naked. For we that are in this tabernacle do groan, being burdened: not for that we would be unclothed, but clothed upon, that mortality might be swallowed up of life.

Now he that hath wrought us for the self-same thing, is God, who also hath given unto us the earnest of the Spirit. Therefore we are always confident, knowing that, while we are at home in the body, we are absent from the Lord. We are confident, I say, and willing rather to be absent from the body, and to be present with the Lord. Wherefore we labor, that, whether present or absent, we may be accepted of him.

For we must all appear before the judgment-seat of Christ; that every one may receive the things done in his body, according to that he hath done, whether it be good or bad. The hour is coming, in the which all that are in the graves shall hear his voice, and shall come forth.

For God hath appointed a day, in the which he will judge the world in righteousness by that man whom he hath ordained; whereof he hath given assurance unto all men, in that he hath raised him from the dead.

But God, who is rich in mercy, for his great love wherewith he loved us, even when we were dead in sins, hath quickened us together with Christ; and hath raised us up together, and made us sit together in heavenly places, in Christ Jesus: that in the ages to come he might show the exceeding riches of his grace, in kindness toward us through Christ Jesus.

RESURRECTION ASSURED.

But I would not have you to be ignorant, brethren, concerning them which are asleep, that ye sorrow not, even as others which have no hope. For I delivered unto you first of all that which I also received, how that Christ died for our sins according to the scriptures; and that he was buried, and that he rose again the third day according to the scriptures.

Now if Christ rose from the dead, how say some among you that there is no resurrection of the dead? But if there be no resurrection of the dead, then is Christ not risen; and if Christ be not raised, your faith is vain; ye are yet in your sins. Then they also which are fallen asleep in Christ are perished. But now is Christ risen from the dead, and become the first-fruits of them that slept: Christ the first-fruits; afterward they that are Christ's at his coming.

For if Jesus died and rose again, even so them also which sleep in Jesus will God bring with him. For this we say unto you by the word of the Lord, that we which are alive and remain unto the coming of the Lord shall not prevent them which are asleep.

For the Lord himself shall descend from heaven with a shout, with the voice of the archangel, and with the trump of God: and the dead in Christ shall rise first: then we which are alive and remain, shall be caught up together with them in the clouds, to meet the Lord in the air: and so shall we ever be with the Lord. Wherefore comfort one another with these words.

But some will say, How are the dead raised up? and with what body do they come?

Thou fool, that which thou sowest is not quickened except it die: and that which thou sowest, thou sowest not that body that shall be, but bare grain; it may chance of wheat, or of some other grain: but God giveth it a body as it hath pleased him, and to every seed his own body.

All flesh is not the same flesh; but there is one flesh of men, another flesh of beasts, another of fishes, and another of birds. There are also celestial bodies, and bodies terrestrial: but the glory of the celestial is one, and the glory of the terrestrial is another.

There is one glory of the sun, and another glory of the moon, and another glory of the stars; for star differeth from star in glory.

So also is the resurrection of the dead. It is sown in corruption, it is raised in incorruption: sown in dishonor; raised in glory: sown in weakness; raised in power: sown a natural body; raised a spiritual body. There is a natural body, and there is a spiritual body.

Howbeit that was not first which is spiritual, but that which is natural; and afterward that which is spiritual. The first man is of the earth, earthy: the second man is the Lord from heaven. And as we have borne the image of the earthy, we shall also bear the image of the heavenly.

Now this I say brethren: that flesh and blood cannot inherit the kingdom of God; neither doth corruption inherit incorruption. Behold, I show you a mystery: We shall not all sleep, but we shall all be changed, in a moment, in the twinkling of an eye, at the last trump:

for the trumpet shall sound, and the dead shall be raised incorruptible, and we shall be changed. For this corruptible must put on incorruption, and this mortal must put on immortality.

So when this corruptible shall have put on incorruption, and this mortal shall have put on immortality, then shall be brought to pass the saying that is written, Death is swallowed up in victory. O death, where is thy sting? O grave, where thy victory?

The sting of death is sin; and the strength of sin is the law. But thanks be to God, which giveth us the victory through our Lord Jesus Christ. Therefore, my beloved brethren, be ye steadfast, unmovable, always abounding in the work of the Lord, forasmuch as ye know that your labor is not in vain in the Lord.

BLESSING, and honor, and glory, and power, be unto Him that sitteth upon the throne, and unto the Lamb, for ever and ever.

When the Son of man shall come in his glory, and all the holy angels with him, then shall he sit upon the throne of his glory: and before him shall be gathered all nations: and he shall separate them one from another, as a shepherd divideth his sheep from the goats: and he shall set the sheep on his right hand, but the goats on the left.

Then shall the King say unto them on his right hand: Come, ye blessed of my Father, inherit the kingdom prepared for you from the foundation of the world: for I was an hungered, and ye gave me meat: I was thirsty, and ye gave me drink: I was a stranger, and ye took me in: naked, and ye clothed me: I was sick, and ye visited me: I was in prison, and ye came unto me.

Then shall the righteous answer him, saying: Lord, when saw we thee an hungered, and fed thee? or thirsty, and gave thee drink? When saw we thee a stranger, and took thee in? or naked, and clothed thee? Or when saw we thee sick, or in prison, and came unto thee?

And the King shall answer and say unto them, Verily I say unto you, inasmuch as ye have done it unto one of the least of these my brethren, ye have done it unto me.

WATCHFUL WAITING.

Wherefore, beloved, seeing that ye look for such things, be diligent that ye may be found of him in peace, without spot and blameless, that when his glory shall be revealed, ye may be glad also with exceeding joy.

And the Lord make you to increase and abound in love one toward another, and toward all men, to the end he may stablish your hearts unblamable in holiness before God, even our Father, at the coming of our Lord Jesus Christ with all his saints, when he shall come to be glorified in his saints, and to be admired in all them that believe.

For yet a little while, and he that shall come will come, and will not tarry. Remember now thy Creator in the days of thy youth, while the evil days come not, nor the years draw nigh, when thou shalt say, I have no pleasure in them. While the sun, or the light, or the moon, or the stars, be not darkened, nor the clouds return after the rain: in the day when the keepers of the house shall tremble, and the strong men shall bow themselves, and the grinders cease because they are few, and those that look out of the windows be darkened, and the doors shall be shut in the streets, when the sound of the grinding is low, and he shall rise up at the voice of the bird, and all the daughters of music shall be brought low; when they shall be afraid of that which is high, and fears shall be in the way, and the almond tree shall flourish, and the grasshopper shall be a burden, and desire shall fail: because man goeth to his long home, and the mourners go about the streets: or ever the silver cord be loosed, or the golden bowl be broken, or the pitcher be broken at the fountain, or the wheel broken at the cistern. Then shall the dust return to the earth as it was: and the spirit shall return unto God who gave it. Whatsoever thy hand findeth to do, do it with thy might; for there is no work, nor device, nor knowledge, nor wisdom, in the grave, whither thou goest. Let us hear the conclusion of the whole matter: Fear God, and keep his commandments: for God shall bring every work into judgment, with every secret thing, whether it be good, or whether it be evil.

BUT of that day and that hour knoweth no man, no, not the angels which are in heaven, neither the Son, but the Father. Take ye heed, watch and pray: for ye know not when the time is. Watch, therefore: for ye know not what hour your Lord doth come: at even, or at midnight, or at the cockcrowing, or in the morning: lest coming suddenly he find you sleeping. And what I say unto you I say unto all, Watch.

If the good man of the house had known in what watch the thief would come, he would have watched, and would not have suffered his house to be broken up. Therefore be ye also ready: for in such an hour as ye think not the Son of man cometh. For so an entrance shall be ministered unto you abundantly into the everlasting kingdom of our Lord and Saviour Jesus Christ.

Now unto him that is able to do exceeding abundantly above all that we ask or think, according to the power that worketh in us, unto him be glory in the church by Christ Jesus throughout all ages, world without end. Amen.

SUFFERING SAINTS GLORIFIED.

And I heard a voice from heaven, saying unto me, Write, Blessed are the dead which die in the Lord from henceforth: yea, saith the Spirit, that they may rest from their labors; and their works do follow them.

BLESSED are the poor in spirit: for theirs is the kingdom of heaven.

Blessed are they that mourn: for they shall be comforted.

Blessed are the meek: for they shall inherit the earth.

Blessed are they which do hunger and thirst after righteousness: for they shall be filled.

Blessed are the merciful: for they shall obtain mercy.

Blessed are the pure in heart: for they shall see God.

Blessed are the peacemakers: for they shall be called the children of God.

Blessed are they which are persecuted for righteousness' sake: for theirs is the kingdom of heaven.

AFTER this I beheld, and, lo, a great multitude, which no man could number, of all nations, and kindreds,

and people, and tongues, stood before
the throne, and before the Lamb,
clothed with white robes, and palms
in their hands; and cried with a loud
voice, saying, Salvation to our God
which sitteth upon the throne, and
unto the Lamb.

And one of the elders answered,
saying unto me, What are these
which are arrayed in white robes? and
whence came they? And I said unto
him, Sir, thou knowest. And he said
to me,

These are they which came out of
great tribulation, and have washed
their robes and made them white in
the blood of the Lamb. Therefore
are they before the throne of God,
and serve him day and night in his
temple: and he that sitteth on the
throne shall dwell among them. They
shall hunger no more, neither thirst
any more; neither shall the sun light
on them, nor any heat. For the Lamb,
which is in the midst of the throne,
shall feed them, and shall lead them
unto living fountains of water: and
God shall wipe away all tears from

their eyes. And there shall be no more death, neither sorrow, nor crying, neither shall there be any more pain: for the former things are passed away.

And I heard a great voice out of heaven, saying, Behold, the tabernacle of God is with men, and he will dwell with them, and they shall be his people, and God himself shall be with them, and be their God. And they shall see his face; and his name shall be in their foreheads. And there shall be no night there; and they need no candle, neither light of the sun; for the Lord God giveth them light: and they shall reign for ever and ever.

UNTO him that loved us, and washed us from our sins in his own blood, and hath made us kings and priests unto God and his Father; to him be glory and dominion for ever and ever. Amen.

AND he that sat upon the throne said, Behold, I make all things new. He that overcometh shall inherit all things; and I will be his God, and he shall be my son. Behold, I come quickly; and my reward is with me, to give every man according as his work shall be. Blessed are they that do his commandments, that they may have right to the tree of life, and may enter in through the gates into the city.

And the Spirit and the bride say, Come. And let him that heareth say, Come. And let him that is athirst, come: and whosoever will, let him take the water of life freely. He which testifieth these things saith, Surely I come quickly. Amen. Even so, come, Lord Jesus.

Now the God of peace, that brought again from the dead our Lord Jesus, that great Shepherd of the sheep, through the blood of the everlasting covenant, make you perfect in every good work to do his will, working in you that which is well-pleasing in his sight, through Jesus Christ; to whom be glory for ever and ever. Amen.

ETERNAL REST AND PEACE.

The Lord is my shepherd; I shall not want. He maketh me to lie down in green pastures: he leadeth me beside the still waters. He restoreth my soul: he leadeth me in the paths of righteousness for his name's sake.

Yea, though I walk through the valley of the shadow of death, I will fear no evil: for thou art with me; thy rod and thy staff, they comfort me. Thou preparest a table before me in the presence of mine enemies: thou anointest my head with oil; my cup runneth over.

Surely goodness and mercy shall follow me all the days of my life: and I will dwell in the house of the Lord for ever.

THE LORD bless thee, and keep thee:

The Lord make his face shine upon thee, and be gracious unto thee:

The Lord lift up his countenance upon thee, and give thee peace.

www.ingramcontent.com/pod-product-compliance
Lightning Source LLC
Chambersburg PA
CBHW030851270326
41928CB00008B/1328